THE SOCIAL UNCONSCIOUS
IN PERSONS, GROUPS,
AND SOCIETIES

NEW INTERNATIONAL LIBRARY OF GROUP ANALYSIS

Series Editor: Earl Hopper

Other titles in the Series include:

THE SOCIAL UNCONSCIOUS IN PERSONS, GROUPS, AND SOCIETIES

Volume 2:
Mainly Foundation Matrices

Edited by

Earl Hopper and Haim Weinberg

KARNAC

First published in 2016 by
Karnac Books Ltd
118 Finchley Road, London NW3 5HT

British Library Cataloguing in Publication Data

A C.I.P. for this book is available from the British Library

ISBN 978 1 78220 185 4

Edited, designed and produced by The Studio Publishing Services Ltd
www.publishingservicesuk.co.uk
e-mail: studio@publishingservicesuk.co.uk

Printed in Great Britain by TJ International Ltd, Padstow, Cornwall

www.karnacbooks.com

CONTENTS

ACKNOWLEDGEMENTS

As the Editors of this second volume in the series *The Social Unconscious in Persons, Groups, and Societies,* we are pleased to acknowledge the help and stimulation provided through dialogue with our network of colleagues who are interested in developing our field theory of the social unconscious and its applications to the study of societies. This network is growing in size and international scope. Our multiple *foci* of interests include the mundane elements of our existence, as well as the traumatic pains associated with transgenerational social trauma, and those aspects of our lives that can be modified through clinical work, as well as those that seem to be intractable and recalcitrant. As always, we are grateful to our families and friends for their tolerance of our continuing preoccupations. Céline Stakol has carried the burden of the administrative and technical demands of our labour, and we thank her for this.

Earl Hopper, PhD
Haim Weinberg, PhD

Hanni Biran, MA, is a clinical psychologist, psychoanalyst, and group analyst in private practice in Israel. A supervisor and training psychoanalyst for the Tel-Aviv Institute of Contemporary Psychoanalysis, she teaches at many institutions in Israel and lectures internationally. She is a member of Psycho-Active (an organisation of mental health professionals for the promotion of human rights and against the occupation). Born in Israel to a family of Iranian origin, she is married, with two children and three grandchildren.

Alan Corbett, DClinSci, is a psychoanalytical therapist in private practice in London. A trustee of the Institute of Psychotherapy and Disability, and a member of the Training Committee of the Guild of Psychotherapists, he is a former Director of Respond, and Clinical Director of the CARI (Children at Risk in Ireland) Foundation and ICAP (Immigrant Counselling and Psychotherapy). He is a training therapist and supervisor, and a consultant to many psychotherapy organisations in Britain and Ireland.

Tamsin Cottis, CertEd, MA, UKCP, is an integrative arts child psychotherapist working in schools and in private practice in London, specialising in psychotherapy for people with learning disabilities. She is co-founder and former Assistant Director of Respond, a founder member of the Institute of Psychotherapy and Disability, Consultant Clinical Supervisor at Respond, and a teacher at the Bowlby Centre for Attachment-Based Psychotherapy. Tamsin is a published author of short fiction.

Stephen Frosh, PhD, is Pro-Vice-Master at Birkbeck, University of London, and Professor in the Department of Psychosocial Studies there. Previously Vice-Dean in the Child and Family department at the Tavistock Clinic, London, he has published widely on psychosocial studies, psychoanalysis and social theory.

Earl Hopper, PhD, is a psychoanalyst, group analyst, and organisational consultant in private practice in London. A Distinguished Fellow of the American Group Psychotherapy Association, he is a supervisor and training analyst for the Institute of Group Analysis and other psychotherapy organisations in England. He is an Honorary Tutor at the Tavistock and Portman NHS Trust, and a member of the Faculty of the Post-Doctoral Program at Adelphi University, New York. He is a former President of the International Association for Group Psychotherapy and Group Processes (IAGP), and a former Chairman of the Association of Independent Psychoanalysts of the British Psychoanalytical Society. He is the editor of the New International Library of Group Analysis.

Olga Marlin, PhD (in Czech language published as Olga Marlinova), is a psychoanalyst and supervisor in private practice in Prague. She has earned a Certification in Psychoanalysis from the William Alanson White Institute in New York, where she was in private psychoanalytic practice (1973–1994), a Certification in Group Analytic Therapy and Supervision from the Postgraduate Center for Mental Health in New York, and a European Certificate in Psychotherapy. She is the leader of training and supervision groups for psychotherapists, and a lecturer in universities in Finland.

Kaoru Nishimura, MA, is a Senior Associate Professor of Psychology, and Director of the Institute for Advanced Studies of Clinical Psychology, International Christian University, Tokyo, Japan. He is a member of the Board of the Japan Association of Group Psychotherapy, and the Associate Editor of the *Official Journal of the Japan Association of Group Psychotherapy*.

Carla Penna, PhD, is a psychoanalyst and group analyst in private practice in Rio de Janeiro, Brazil. She is a member of Psychoanalytic Circle of Rio de Janeiro, affiliated to International Federation of Psychoanalytic Societies, Former President of Brazilian Association of Group Psychotherapy, and a former President of the Group Analytic Psychotherapy Society of the State of Rio de Janeiro.

Ravit Raufman, PhD, is a clinical psychologist and group psychotherapist in Israel. A senior lecturer and faculty member of the University of Haifa, Israel, she is a member of the Israeli Psychoanalytic Psychotherapy Association.

Haim Weinberg, PhD, is an Israeli psychologist, group analyst, and certified group therapist, living in the USA. He teaches at the Wright Institute, Berkeley, the Alliant International University, Sacramento, and leads a group psychotherapy Doctoral Program at the Professional School of Psychology, Sacramento. He is a former President of the Israeli Group Psychotherapy Association, and of the Northern Group Psychotherapy Society. He has moderated the group psychotherapy discussion list on the Internet for the past twenty years.

Gerhard Wilke, MA Cantab., DipFHE, is a group analyst and organisational consultant. An Associate of Ashridge Business School and a member of the Institute of Group Analysis (London), he teaches and consults internationally and has published widely in the field of the group analytical study of organisations and on leadership. He served on both the GAS Committee and the IAGP Board and specialises in Large Group work.

Ormont

Su -

mai quobe pou E o It² loss

pʰ + Sl. machit

Sllag - quobe

Introduction

In *The Social Unconscious in Persons, Groups, and Societies: Volume 1: Mainly Theory* (Hopper & Weinberg, 2011), the editors and authors defined the concept of the social unconscious and located it within a more general group analytic perspective concerning empirical and clinical work. Having indicated some of the philosophical implications of this perspective, they compared the Foulkesian concept of the social unconscious to that of Pichon-Rivière, the "co-unconscious" of Moreno, and contemporary psycho-dramatists and socio-dramatists, and to the classical concept of the collective unconscious of Jung. Noting that the contemporary conceptualisation of the collective unconscious is very similar to that of the social unconscious, they emphasised that as a "field theory", in the Lewinian sense of the term, the emergent Foulkesian theory of the social unconscious encompassed sociality, relationality, transpersonality, and collectivity within a transgenerational context. Transpersonality implied that the dyad and the more complex social facts and social processes in which the dyad is embedded are co-created (Foulkes & Anthony, 1957; Lewin, 1951).

It was argued that with regard to the study of collectivity, the Foulkesian concept of matrix was more satisfactory than "group-mind" or the Bionian concept of "group-mentality", mainly because, at least in English, the notion of mind and mentality connote "brain" to a much greater extent than either "soul" or "spirit", on the one hand, or "culture", on the other. The notion of group brain implied an excessively strong connection between the neurobiology of the human species and the socio-cultural-political organisation of human groupings. A matrix is a property of a "people" or a plurality of persons, and not a property of a particular social formation, or, more precisely, the matrix has to be understood in terms of its degree of "institutionalisation". What is true of the members of a particular social system is not necessarily true of the social system itself, whether a group or a society. It was emphasised that in the study of the social unconscious, social trauma is of particular importance, for several reasons: processes of failed dependency and loss are closely associated with all processes of internalisation, traumatic anxieties urge towards the transgenerational repetition and transmission of the traumatic experiences in which they originate, and social trauma is a manifestation of the vulnerability of all human bonds and links. Although the chapters in the first volume of this series barely traced the contours of the concept of the social unconscious and the theory in which it is embedded, they have stimulated a great deal of intellectual activity, as seen in a spate of articles (e.g., Scholz, 2014; Taha, 2014; Tubert-Oklander & Hernandez-Tubert, 2014a,b,c) and workshops (e.g., "Studies of large groups and the social unconscious" in Belgrade, 2013 and "Learning through experience: inclusion/exclusion phenomena in and between the traditions of Bion, Foulkes, and Main" in Belgrade, 2014.) In fact, colleagues who are contributing to this series have presented work on the social unconscious in virtually all of the recent group psychotherapy conferences. Some of this work is being developed into chapters for subsequent volumes.

We believe that while this work is still in incubation, it is imperative to publish several empirical studies of various aspects of the social unconscious with special reference to the foundation matrices of several "peoples" in their contextual societies. Many colleagues and students have requested more examples of the basic arguments concerning the social unconscious, especially the importance of social trauma and the centrality of myths. Thus, Volume 2 in the series on the study of what has come to be known as "the social unconscious" is sub-titled "Mainly Foundation Matrices".

As a basic guide to these empirical studies of foundation matrices, it is worth quoting extensively from the developing work of Foulkes, as reported in "Group-analytic contexts", March 2014, pp. 40–42. These quotations indicate the centrality of the concept of matrix in group analytical thinking as well as the search for explanatory metaphors, starting with the body and the brain, but shifting towards systems thinking more generally:

1. The social matrix can be thought of as a network in quite the same way as the brain is a network of fibres and cells, which together form a complex unit . . . [I]ts lines of force may be conceived of as passing right through the individual members and may therefore be called a transpersonal network, comparable to a magnetic field. (Foulkes & Anthony, 1957, pp. 258–260)

2. . . . it is always the transpersonal network that is sensitised and gives utterance or responds. In this sense we can postulate the existence of a group mind (Foulkes, 1964, p. 181)

3. The matrix is the hypothetical web of communication and relationship in a given group. [U]ltimately [it] determines the meaning and significance of all events. [A]ll communication and interpretations, verbal and non-verbal, rest [upon it] . . . Inside this network the individual is conceived as a nodal point. The individual . . . is not conceived as a closed but as an open system. . . . As is the case of the neurone in the nervous system so is the individual suspended in the group matrix. (Foulkes, 1964, p. 118)

4. This complex network of relations, norms and values, and systems of communication . . . is called [a] "matrix", because it is the mother-soil in which all dynamic processes take their place. . . . [I]t is possible to claim a firm pre-existing community or communion between the members, founded eventually upon the fact that they are all human . . . [And thus] . . . have the same qualities . . . the same anatomy and physiology, and also perhaps the same archaic traces of ancient experiences [as all the other members of the species]. (Foulkes, 1971, p. 6)

5. . . . A good deal of what is usually called external or social is at the same time deeply internal and [a] very powerful dynamic influence [on] the total being as he develops. This comprises our social (and) cultural . . . inheritances transmitted over generations, even for the building up of one's own image of one's body . . . There are some basic things shared by our groups even before the individual members have met, such as language, the particular culture,

even class and education. This is called the Foundation Matrix. [It is the] . . . common ground [which the members bring] . . . into the group. What we traditionally look upon as the innermost self, the intra-psychic as against the external world, is thus not only share-able, but is in fact already shared. . . . Apart from this fundamen-tally shared life we can see this matrix growing and developing more and more, embracing more and more complex issues which are very important for the therapeutic process altogether. This, which develops under our own eyes, is called the Dynamic Matrix. All mental processes, including of course all therapeutic ones, take place in this hypothetical web of communication or communion, in this matrix. (Foulkes, 1975, p. 65)

As the custodians of the *New Dictionary of Concepts in Group Analysis*, under the leadership of Soeren Aagard (2014), have written,

Foulkes chose the word "matrix" deliberately, because of [its] deriva-tion from "mother" (matrix means uterus in Latin). This gives the matrix a human frame of reference, a metaphor of nurture and growth. For Foulkes, the matrix is a description of the inter-subjective field within a group. Foulkes suggests (that) there exists within a group a "field effect", or "atmosphere", which is not consciously known, but which nevertheless connects people. He makes a distinc-tion between the template of relationships [from the contextual soci-ety], which is laid down in the [family of orientation], calling it the "foundation matrix", and the "dynamic matrix" which [develops] in the analytic group. The matrix can be thought of as operating on two levels, the "foundation matrix" which is created by the features common to the members from the start, and the "dynamic matrix", the flow of themes, exchanges and events which materialize as the group develops in intimacy and maturity . . . with its potential for growth and change. The personality is formed within the foundation matrix of early relationships, and it . . . follows that there is a possibility of change in the dynamic matrix of the experiential group. (pp. 40–42)

Many other quotations from the work of Foulkes and his collabo-rators and other group analysts might be cited to this general effect, especially in the context of social philosophy and the social sciences in the nineteenth and early twentieth centuries, both in Europe and in the USA. It is still relevant at least to mention the work of Marx, Weber, Durkheim, and Tonnies. However, going beyond the evolu-tionary and revolutionary preoccupations of nineteenth-century social scientists, the construction of theoretical models and conceptual schemes for the comparative study of social systems was one of the main concerns of modern sociology and social psychology. Many scholars have argued that it is essential to distinguish conceptually biological, social, cultural, and communicational structures and dimensions, which are, in empirical reality, completely intertwined. Some social scientists have referred to patterns of interaction, normation, and communication, as well as to economic, technological, and political dimensions of social reality. In the tradition of group analysis specifically, de Maré (1972) distinguished "structure", "process", and "content". Hopper (2003) defined "social system" as distinct from system more generally, and specified several dimensions of social systems that could be used in the comparative study of them. Hopper argued that, as a contextual discipline, the focus of group analysis would always be on "open" systems. However, as late as 1994, Brown and Zinkin observed that the theoretical basis of the concept of the foundation matrix, as ". . . laid down by its initiator, S. H. Foulkes involves the recognition of the deeply social nature of the human personality".

The problem has been, and continues to be, that despite these intimations of theoretical models and conceptual schemes for the comparative study of foundation matrices, or even the study in depth of any one of them, much of this work has proved to be too abstract and too general to offer more than a guideline, or perhaps a checklist, concerning the basic social, cultural, and communicational phenomena that must be taken into account. It is for this reason that we continue to be engaged in the development of more sophisticated and pragmatic models for the study of foundation matrices specifically and for the study of the social unconscious in general. We hope that these efforts will illustrate the old adage that there is nothing so practical as a good theory. Meanwhile . . .

This volume is divided into two parts. The first part consists of three chapters concerning the study of myths, which are an important element in the cultural dimension of the foundation matrices of all societies. In the first chapter, Stephen Frosh discusses the vicissitudes of the myth of Isaac's binding, the "Aqidah", throughout the history of the Jewish people. He focuses on transgenerational transmission of memories of historical events, especially those that were traumatic. Such processes of cultural transmission are central to the study of the

social unconscious, because they parallel those of biological reproduction and the genetic transmission. A full appreciation of the importance of cultural transmission allows us to avoid the Lamarckian
fallacy that experience becomes coded in the germ cells.

In Chapter Two, Hanni Biran discusses the myth of the Tower of
Babel in terms of the perspective of Bion, Foulkes, and Jung, as well
as the work of Hopper and Lawrence with respect to processes of
incohesion. Biran describes some of the social implications of this
myth, for example, the pattern of relationships among societal sub-
groups and contra-groups in Israel in the context of the idealising
ideology of the "melting pot".

In Chapter Three, Ravit Raufman examines some of the meanings
of traditional folk-tales of the Druze community in terms of their social
unconscious. Raufman focuses on a well known tale, "The Wolf and
the Kids", and explains the relationship between the "local" foundation matrix of the Druze society and the "universal" foundation matrix
of other societies in which this myth can be found, the former akin to
the social unconscious, with its emphasis on society and culture, the
latter to the collective unconscious, with its emphasis on species.

The second part of this book describes and analyses the foundation
matrices of people from specific societies. In Chapter Four, Gerhard
Wilke describes the restraints and constraints of social, cultural, and
communicational arrangements of which German people tend to be
unaware. He focuses on the second and third generation of children
of Nazi parents and Holocaust perpetrators in the context of post
Second World War Germany as a traumatised society. He emphasises
the centrality of social trauma in the study of the social unconscious
and the foundation matrix.

In Chapter Five, Olga Marlin examines that foundation matrix of
post Second World War Czech society in the context of two massive
social traumas in the twentieth century, one stemming from the Nazi
occupation, and the second from the Soviet totalitarian regime. She
analyses the foundation matrix in terms of Bion's three basic assumptions, and Hopper's fourth basic assumption of Incohesion. She argues
that in order to function in the totalitarian system, people had to sacrifice their individual autonomy in the context of fear and helplessness,
suppressing their natural assertiveness, initiative, and responsibility,
thus illustrating the recursive nature of social and personal trauma
across the generations.

In Chapter Six, Kaoru Nishimura examines some of the contemporary manifestations of the social unconscious in Japan. Nishimura tracks the long history of Japan as a country who has always adopted and "borrowed" elements from various cultures, often losing its own social identity in the process. This is connected with self-sacrifice as one of the main threads in the foundation matrix of the Japanese people, resulting in the actions of *seppuku* or *hara-kiri*, *kamikaze*, and the spirit of *mujo* (accepting an unchangeable reality). The trauma of the Second World War, including the atomic bomb and the military defeat in general, left the Japanese people feeling ashamed and guilty. This has found continuing expression in popular art and films. The decision to set up nuclear power plants in a country stricken by earthquakes, and the general response to nuclear disasters, must be understood in this context.

In Chapter Seven, Alan Corbett and Tamsin Cottis describe social attitudes in Britain and Ireland towards people who are intellectually disabled. The authors argue that the history of trauma in Ireland, as an invaded, colonised, and virtually starved country, is an essential element in its foundation matrix, and that this pattern of social trauma informs the treatment of the intellectually disabled. These processes are located within the context of the religious system of Ireland as well as its system of social and economic stratification and history of colonial subjugation.

In the final chapter, Carla Penna analyses the foundation matrix of the many peoples of Brazil. This country has always fascinated the "Western mind", and has often been used as an illustration of the creation myth of "Earthly Paradise". Penna focuses on the miscegenation process, and the co-created character types of the "cordial man", the "rogue", and the "mulatto".

The authors of these chapters have worked and written as "participant observers" in and of their respective societies. Each would acknowledge that it is extremely difficult and often very painful to become conscious, or, at least, more fully conscious, of these social cultural and political arrangements. After all, there are reasons why most people are unconscious and preconscious of such arrangements, in the sense that they have repressed and/or denied and split off their knowledge and implicit memories of them. A fuller appreciation of their defensive and protective functions is inevitably associated with the experience or re-experience of traumatic anxieties, and, possibly, with social and political action. We will continue to explore these issues in subsequent volumes.

References

Aagard, S. (2014). Group analytic concepts: the matrix. *Group Analytic Contexts, March*(63): 40–42.

Brown, D., & Zinkin, L. (Eds.) (1994). *The Psyche and the Social World*. London: Routledge.

De Maré, P. (1972). *Perspectives in Group Psychotherapy*. London: Allen & Unwin.

Foulkes, S. H. (1964). *Therapeutic Group Analysis*. London: Allen and Unwin [reprinted London: Karnac, 1984].

Foulkes, S. H. (1971). Access to unconscious processes in the group-analytic group. *Group Analysis, 4*: 4–14.

Foulkes, S. H. (1975). A short outline of the therapeutic processes in group-analytic psychotherapy. *Group Analysis, 8*, 63–69.

Foulkes, S. H., & Anthony, E. J. (1957). *Group Psychotherapy* (1st edn). London: Penguin.

Foulkes, S. H., & Anthony, E. J. (1965). *Group Psychotherapy* (2nd edn). London: Penguin.

Hopper, E. (2003). A sociological view of large groups. In: *The Social Unconscious: Selected Papers*. London: Jessica Kingsley.

Hopper, E., & Weinberg, H. (Eds.) (2011). *The Social Unconscious in Persons, Groups and Societies: Volume 1: Mainly Theory*. London: Karnac.

Lewin, K. (1951). *Field Theory in Social Science*. New York: Harper Bros.

Scholz, R. (2014). (Foundation-) matrix reloaded—some remarks on a useful concept and its pitfalls. *Group Analysis, 47*(3): 201–212.

Taha, M. (2014). Social positions, scripts and functioning dynamics: phenomenology of the Egyptian social unconscious. *International Journal of Group Psychotherapy, 64*(3): 323–344.

Tubert–Oklander, J., & Hernandez–Tubert, R. (2014a). The social unconscious and the large group Part I: The British and the Latin American traditions. *Group Analysis, 47*(2): 99–112.

Tubert–Oklander, J., & Hernandez–Tubert, R. (2014b). The social unconscious and the large group Part II: A context that becomes a text. *Group Analysis, 47*(3): 329–344.

Tubert–Oklander, J., & Hernandez–Tubert, R. (2014c). The social unconscious and the large group Part III: Listening to the voices in the wind. *Group Analysis, 47*(4): 420–435.

PART I

MYTHS

I love this article, partly
bec. it's beautifully written,
but mostly bec. it chimes
w much with my view about
the place of violence &
murder as a foundling
fantasy, memory, anchoring
in the "historical" frame of
a people/society, heavily
allus = the SU. And, more
specifically, that it links
with the work on the killing
of the primal father —

Makes me think of
foundational any art
= GA —
= the primal complex the
= the slaying of the mother v
  father   if not
                              P₂

— the traumas of
  birth & death
— the drama
  attached to separation
— the inevitability of
  loss —
  " the inheritance
    of loss!"

CHAPTER ONE

Born with a knife in their hearts: transmission, trauma, identity, and the social unconscious*

Stephen Frosh

The history of a trauma

The question of what passes between people over time is one that should lie close to the heart of any group psychology. What is it that is passed down from one generation to another, what draws us to those who came before and makes us invest in those who come after? With whom are we affiliated, to whom are we indebted, what is it that we carry, unremarked sometimes, but very often re-enacted, from those who have experienced the critical events that we remember as history, or perhaps as an echo to which we attune ourselves, not quite sure of what it is we hear? The question is how *transmission* occurs: we know something is preserved of the past, whether we want it to be or not, but how does this take place?

Clearly, there are explicit teachings that each generation tries to communicate to the next, maybe even to impose on them. Teachers and parents take this to be their task. But there is another kind of transmission that goes along with, underpins, and sometimes

---

* This chapter is adapted from Stephen Frosh, *Hauntings: Psychoanalysis and Ghostly Transmissions*. London: Palgrave, 2013.

bypasses these overt mechanisms, even undermining them. This kind of transmission is of something unspoken—one has to call it *unconscious*, despite all the complications of that label—with which we find ourselves invested or burdened. Without knowing it, that is, we are revenants, repeating without necessarily remembering or working through. We could say that the terminology here is that of ghosts and haunting. It clearly resonates with the idea of a social unconscious (Hopper, 2003), most forcefully in the sense of a matrix promoting intersubjective sharing between groups of people (or within "a people") within the frame of cultural inheritance. That is to say, we are in the realm of something seemingly intangible that nevertheless has widespread effects over time and space, whether we like it or not. In his famous 1926 letter to the Bnai Brith, Freud describes his lack of overt Jewish affiliation yet states his irrepressible pull towards Jewish identity in a language that also hints that what is most inexpressible is most powerful. Symptomatically perhaps, because Jewishness aroused Freud's ambivalence and was a special kind of concern for him, this is the only occasion on which he uses the term "identity" (Grinberg & Grinberg, 1974).

> But there remained enough to make the attraction of Judaism and the Jews irresistible, many dark emotional powers all the stronger the less they could be expressed in words, as well as the clear consciousness of an inner identity, the familiarity of the same psychological structure. (E. Freud, 1961, p. 368)

It is this pull, this identity built out of an inarticulate kind of memory, that is expressed in cultural and personal transmission. Yerushalmi (1991, p. 31) calls it "a trilling wire in the blood".

Intergenerational haunting was a primary concern of Freud's late social texts, and particularly *Moses and Monotheism* (1939a), which was written as the "old world" was destroyed in the 1930s. Jacqueline Rose (2007, p. 84) makes the first important link here. She writes,

> We could say that the question of his Jewish identity propels Freud towards the idea of "transgenerational haunting", a concept forged by the Hungarian émigré analysts Maria Torok and Nicolas Abraham, significantly in the aftermath of this historical moment, as they tried to understand the silent persistence of the Holocaust in the minds of second-generation Jews.

Certainly the issue of Jewish identity is at the centre of much of
Freud's thinking in the period in which he wrote *Moses and Monotheism*, precisely the period of the gathering storm of Nazism. But for
the moment it is another track that is suggested by this concatenation
of transference and transgenerational haunting: that is, the question of
what happens to traumatic experiences. As Rose notes, the origins of
Abraham and Torok's (1986, 1994) theorisation of cryptography is the
question of how the Holocaust persists in the mind. This has continued to be a major issue for those working with second-generation
survivors and also, more tentatively and, at times, apologetically, the
children of perpetrators. It is not just the Holocaust, of course, though
this is the key modern trauma for Jews and for intellectuals trying to
make sense of the triumph of barbarism; it is all trauma in every place
that it appears, in all acts of personal violence and political oppression, of colonialism and genocide, of sexual and racial hatred, of the
occlusion of historical wrongs and the persistence of their return.
Transference occurs in the consulting room as something in the
personal relationship between patient and analyst. But transference is
also transmission; it is the present chained to the past, not knowing
what puppet master is pulling the strings.

This is clearly in some way an account of the history of trauma as
it becomes personalised and reproduced from one generation to the
next. "The very thing that provokes the worst suffering must be kept
alive", Derrida states (1986, p. xxxv), putting his finger on a recurrent
problem in comprehending intergenerational transmission as well as
personal psychic suffering. Why is it that so much of one generation's
life is spent managing the difficulties of the previous one? Is there an
unconscious form of transmission—a haunting—that is embedded in
the notion of transference and that inescapably both lies at the heart
of trauma and also of the inheritance of identity? It certainly seems
implicit in Freud's formulation of how the concerns of one generation
structure those of another: "the super-ego arises", he writes (Freud,
1923b, p. 54), "as we know, from an identification with the father taken
as a model". What hides in the mind, judging and at times persecuting, is derived from an intergenerational identification. Elsewhere
(Freud, 1930a) it becomes clear that it is the *authority* of the father—
the child's fantasy of the father's superego—that is the source of the
child's superego. Which is to say, we are haunted by what haunts
those who came before.

Analysts and others since Freud have emphasised the way in which trauma acts as a kind of fixation, in which the unsymbolised past invades the present, giving life its backward temporality. Volkan (2002, p. 45) describes the swamping of temporal space as "time collapse", denoting by this "the conscious and unconscious connections between past trauma and present threat that typically emerge when a chosen trauma is powerfully reactivated". There is an event, and it is traumatic because it is not recognised as such but becomes repressed and silenced. It is inaccessible, yet it continues to operate; the psyche wrestles with it and unconsciously identifies with it. When it occurs, its significance passes the subject by, but later, it cannot be avoided, it keeps cropping up, and yet is nowhere to be found. If one thinks about this schematically, it becomes clear that what is being described is some kind of crisis that creates the structure within which later events take place. The backwards referentiality, the becoming-real that is only possible because an original act has been occluded and foreclosed, is exactly what makes society function. This is perhaps one of the things that Freud (1912–1913) was getting at with his idea of the killing of the primal father: a repressed secret is necessary for the founding of society; because this secret is shared (in his account, between the "brothers") it also generates feelings of guilt. Seeing psychoanalysis as a therapeutic social intervention, Freud aims to draw attention to this secret and bring it into the light of reason. As Rose (2007, p. 78) puts it in relation to *Moses and Monotheism*, Freud wanted "the Jewish people, and through them all people, to imagine the unimaginable – to contemplate the possibility that the most binding social ties are forged through an act of violence". What kind of violence would this be? Freud's answer is characteristic of someone steeped in concerns over authority, power and betrayal: "It seems to me a most surprising discovery that the problems of social psychology, too, should prove soluble on the basis of one single concrete point – man's relation to his father" (1912–1913, p. 157).

The cultural inheritance of paternal violence

In the context of his attempt to explain the continuing pull of Jewish identity, Freud's (1939a) account of the passing on of paternal violence (and violence against the father) is centred on the story of Moses. His

idea is that the traumatic killing of Moses by the Jewish people underpins the iterated experience of Jewish identity formation throughout
later generations. The argument here is that there is something in the
narrative that binds a people together, as if the group draws on a
founding myth in order to reconcile itself with its situation, constantly
reinterpreting but also reusing that myth as a guide to the meaning of
its experiences. The myth is consequently a paradigm for action, but
also for understanding what the world might be about, and, because
of this, it is a powerful reference point for identity formation. In group
analytic terms, such founding myths might be seen as the foundation
matrix of a culture, the taken-for-granted but consciously and unconsciously drawn on kernel of meaning that gives shared experience its
shape.

While Freud's paradigmatic Biblical figure is Moses, there is a
more obvious invocation and exploration of paternal violence in the
Bible, one which has been both consciously and unconsciously utilised
by Jews in order to make sense of later trauma. The primary father, at
least for the Jews, was Abraham, and the foundational story is that of
the "Binding of Isaac" (Genesis 22). The narrative runs as follows.
Abraham has just about put all his complex affairs in order and seems
to be settled in the land of the Philistines. He has had two children in
his old age. One of them, Ishmael, born of a maidservant, has been
sent into the wilderness; the other one, Isaac, the child of Abraham's
wife, Sarah, is to be his successor, through whom God's promise of
future fertility is to be fulfilled. Out of nowhere ("after these things"—
verse 1) God speaks to Abraham and demands that he take Isaac to
Mount Moriah, three days' journey away, and offer him up there as a
burnt offering. Abraham does this without question, and Isaac com-
plies. When they are on the mountain alone together, Abraham binds
Isaac tightly to a pile of wood (hence the name "binding" or "Akedah"
for this event) and takes a knife to slay him. At that moment, an angel
intervenes, commanding (verse 12), "Abraham, Abraham, lay not
your hand on the lad, nor do anything to him". Abraham desists
and then has his attention drawn by the angel to a ram caught in a
thicket by its horns. He releases Isaac and sacrifices the ram instead,
for which reason Jews use a ram's horn as a shofar, or trumpet, on
Rosh Hashanah, the New Year.

This story, which is absolutely central to Jewish readings of
Abraham as a man of ideal and unbounded faith, is also important in

a different version for Moslems. The Akedah is iconic in western culture, too, and not only because Christianity treated it as a fore-runner of the Golgotha story, claiming the actual sacrifice and resurrection of Jesus as superior to the aborted sacrifice of Isaac. For Kierkegaard (quoted in Zornberg, 2009, p. 169), "There were countless generations who knew the story of Abraham by heart, word for word, but how many did it render sleepless?" The horror and disturbance of the piece troubles, it seems, much of the world's dreams. For Jews specifically, the Akedah is an example of a template for intergenerational transmission of trauma and identity. Religiously, it is crucial in marking the confirmation of God's covenant with Abraham. But there is a more sombre resonance of the Akedah too, as the paradigmatic example of how to face the final test of one's existence, which at times of extreme duress has been the model for action by Jews whose lives were threatened. Shalom Spiegel (1967), in his comprehensive account of the Akedah in Jewish history, documents instances in which the readiness of Abraham to sacrifice his son was concretely re-enacted by Jewish communities suffering extreme persecution, notably in Roman and Crusader times—events which are recollected in prayers and lamentations that entered the Jewish canon. For example, Spiegel offers liturgical material from the time of the Crusades that uses the Akedah as a motif, often implicitly or explicitly posing a direct question: why, when God was moved to save one person, did He do nothing when so many were murdered? Spiegel points out how this material not only draws on the Akedah but also suggests that the generations faced by these massacres saw themselves as having undergone a greater trial than Abraham: "Ask ye now, and see, was there ever such a holocaust as this *since the days of Adam*?" (pp. 19–20). Adam, not Abraham; that is, this tragedy was greater than that of the Akedah.

The model of Abraham's behaviour as the father who would actually have killed his son is exactly the model that some—perhaps many—took. Spiegel gives several examples, including one from Worms, where 800 Jews died in two days of destruction in 1096. The records describe how Meshullam, a respected member of the besieged community, took his son and called out, "All ye great and small, hearken unto me. Here is my son whom God gave me and to whom my wife Zipporah gave birth *in her old age* , Isaac is the child's name; and now I shall offer him up as Father *Abraham offered up his son Isaac*".

Zipporah then intervened to try to stop the killing: "O my lord, my lord, *do not lay thy hand upon the lad* . . ." But the father did not stop: "*And he bound his son Isaac, and picked up the knife to slay his son*, and recited the blessing appropriate for slaughter. And the lad replied, 'Amen'. And the father slew the lad" (Spiegel, p. 24). Meshullam and his wife then ran out and were murdered. Among the many striking things about this documentary record is the direct use of the exact words from the Biblical account (italicised in the quotation); the Akedah becomes a template for the sacrifice of the son. Of course, there is a difference in that the boy is killed by his father to prevent him falling into the hands of the mob, but it is also a religious act, both a cry of a helpless father for God to intervene and stop the murder as he did in the original Akedah, and a way in which the Jews of that time and place set themselves within the narrative trajectory of their traumatic history, starting with the first Jew of all, "Father Abraham". It is also an accusation: "Over such as these, wilt Thou hold Thy peace, O Lord?" (p. 25).

There is a lot of complexity in the attitudes expressed in the material Spiegel presents, some of which are recapitulated in theological responses to the Holocaust. These attitudes range from a passionate indictment of God for not intervening to prevent slaughter, even though loss of *faith* never seems to be an issue, to using the Akedah as the precedent for sacrificing one's son if one has to, hence making the acts of the persecuted generation continuous with those of Abraham. The traditional interpretation, however, is at variance with many of these attitudes. For the classical rabbis, the Akedah should be read first as a test of Abraham's willingness to give up his most precious possession for the sake of God; and second as an injunction *against* child sacrifice. The rabbinic commentators insist that the Akedah demonstrates the *superiority* of Judaism in rejecting the child sacrifices that were common practice among the surrounding peoples of the time. This is no small feat and occurs not without struggle, and the rabbis repeatedly show sensitivity to it. Indeed, they go to great lengths to assert the superiority of animal over human sacrifice, resonating with the psychoanalytic idea of the superiority of the symbolic over the concrete. There is frequent iteration in the rabbinic literature of the idea that, in substituting the ram for Isaac, it is *as though* Isaac has been sacrificed. The ram symbolises Isaac and in this way converts a practice that has become abhorrent into one that is acceptable to God. Spiegel quotes several Talmudic examples on this, concluding (p. 73) that "The Akedah story declared war on *the remnant of idolatry in Israel* and undertook to remove root and branch the whole long, terror-laden inheritance from idolatrous generations".

This much is clear, yet there is evidence that even though the classical view is dominant, traces remain of something else—a tradition that Isaac actually died and was brought back to life. The obvious textual problem that Abraham was prohibited from harming his son is matched by another textual difficulty: what then did happen to Isaac? On the way to the mountain, the text states twice (verses 6 and 8) "they went both of them together". After the Akedah, however, it states (verse 19), "So Abraham returned unto his young men". In the next chapter, when Sarah dies, there is also no mention of Isaac, so what could have happened to him? Spiegel quotes various naturalistic explanations offered by the rabbis (he went by another route, he remained on Mount Moriah for three years until he reached the age of forty, and then he married Rebeccah). But some commentators suggested a more radical solution: Isaac had actually been sacrificed, and, just like the ram, he was awaiting his return to life.

> And Isaac, where was he? The Holy One, blessed be He, brought him into the Garden of Eden, and there he stayed three years . . . R. Judah says: When the sword touched Isaac's throat his soul flew clean out of him. And when He let His voice be heard from between the two cherubim, "Lay not thy hand upon the lad," the lad's soul returned to his body. Then his father unbound him, and Isaac rose, knowing that in this way the dead would come back to life in the future; whereupon he began to recite, Blessed are thou O Lord who quickens the dead. (Spiegel, p. 30)

Some rabbis associated the phrase "one bead of thy necklace" from the Song of Songs (4, 9) with the mark left by the knife on Isaac's neck; an alternative account is that even though Abraham did not slay his son with the knife, he left him to *burn*, reducing him to ashes. Spiegel points out that this would have happened if, after restraining himself, Abraham genuinely did *nothing* to Isaac; as he had already bound him to the burning pyre, "why, in a twinkling the whole pile went up in a blaze and the flames of fire had Isaac to themselves and he was reduced to ashes and dust" (p. 36). There are, indeed, many references to the "ashes of Isaac" in rabbinic literature, for example to explain the custom of putting ashes on the head of a mourner, all of which attest to the continuing echoes of the idea that Isaac was actually sacrificed and then returned to life. The point here is not to re-read the Akedah in opposition to the rabbis: over time, they had their way and symbolism (albeit in the material form of animal sacrifice) triumphed over the desire for human sacrifice. Nevertheless, this seems to have been a hard-won battle and one that perhaps had an ironic turn when later Jews found themselves enacting not the staying of Abraham's hand, but the sacrificial act.

There is a lot more that could be said about the Akedah, and, indeed, there is an immense religious and psychoanalytic literature on the topic, but this is enough for now. The key points are first the residue of paternal violence, and second the way this works through history. On the first, we have sufficient material to suggest that the subjugated narrative of Isaac's actual death survived. Not only has this been picked up in Christianity (which is presumably one reason why it was repressed by Jews), but it is also a genuine element in Jewish myth-making. More psychologically minded commentators also recognise that what is going on in the text is a very difficult and uncertain struggle between the impulse to protect and the impulse to murder. Zornberg (2009) notes that the early rabbinic commentators tell a story of Abraham's youth in which he destroys his father Terach's idols and is put in a furnace by the ruler, Nimrod, as a consequence. Abraham survives this, but his brother, Haran, copying Abraham, does not. Zornberg argues that this is read by the rabbis as the murder of his son by Terach, and that awareness of this as a flaw in paternity is something that haunts Abraham. For the rabbis, this mode of human sacrifice may have been what marked the idolatrous world that Abraham left; for Abraham in the story, the leaving of it was not yet absolutely secure. Zornberg comments,

> In all his apparently random wanderings, he is fated to reach that place. For what has been implanted in him—the father who kills his son—will have to undergo a *test*: something implicit in his past, an "unthought known", will have to be unfolded, lived through in the present, so that it can finally assume its proper place in the past. (Zornberg, 2009, p. 193)

The test, therefore, is of whether Abraham can resolve the violence implicit in fatherhood. In a savage reversal of Freud that is also psychically accurate, the classical commentators understood a father's murderous envy of his sons. Additionally, while it is true that, as a consequence of the Akedah, God's promise of protection to Abraham and his descendants is confirmed, there is also evidence that Abraham is punished for his willingness to revisit the trauma of paternal violence on his child. As scholars have often noted, the shock of the Akedah is such that Abraham's wife Sarah dies when she hears of it, and Abraham himself loses the capacity to talk to God or to his son, for he is never recorded as doing so again. Perhaps his sacrificial zeal is too much for him and his family, and for the interpreters of texts. This is a scandalous reading from the perspective of orthodoxy, but in tune with the psychoanalytic idea that textual traces constantly flag up repressed secrets. This is true, too, for the intergenerational transmission of trauma, where it is the gaps and silences, the obvious bits that are missing from the narratives of lives, that lead younger generations to hunt for the truth or to repeat the trauma.

In addition to this point concerning paternal violence, the second issue relevant to traumatic transmission is about the historical continuity in the story. At times of extreme duress, of which there have been many, Jews have called upon the Akedah and identified themselves with it—or, at least, with the violent, subjugated version in which Isaac actually dies. Of course, this has been to lament and also to avoid what seemed to be worse, the giving-over of children to the murderous mob and the certain death that would then follow anyway, but it is also a psychological and spiritual state of identification that is evoked when the Akedah is called upon in this way. The identification is specifically with the protagonists in the Akedah story, but also with the trauma of history itself, as if to say, "We knew all along that we were likely to be called, and have prepared ourselves for this day. Now we are at one with what has gone before and with what will come later. We know exactly what is hidden away; the beast has broken forth, and is at our throats." Perhaps even more poignant is the suggestion that the trauma symbolised by the Akedah drives an experience of violent suffering that hovers over all Jews, affecting them in traceable, if often complex and hidden, ways. Gouri's (1960) expression of this is named, in English translation, "Heritage":

> Isaac, as the story goes, was not
> sacrificed. He lived for many years, saw

what pleasure had to offer, until his
eyesight dimmed.
But he bequeathed that hour to his
offspring. They are born with a knife in
their hearts.

Inheritance

The example given here is of how a textual "myth" becomes a template for understanding, and even shaping, experience in later generations, a kind of foundational matrix on which members of a culture draw, sometimes knowingly, sometimes unconsciously. One question this raises concerns the mechanism of the kind of cultural transmission described here: how, exactly, does it happen? It might seem relatively straightforward to account for it in terms of explicit communication and identification from parents to children, and also from material practices in the wider society that influence the perceptions and assumptions of each individual in relatively similar ways. If Jews use the Akedah as a template for their response to suffering, it is because of the textual power of the original Biblical material and commentaries and the iterated homilies that result in Abraham being taken as an identificatory model in Jewish culture. There is also a broader point that some fundamental challenges face every human subject and so it should not be surprising if a relatively restricted range of responses to them is uncovered. All humans have to deal with birth, hunger, separation, sex, loss, and death, so it should be no surprise if they develop roughly similar fantasies and material practices to enable them to do so.

Freud (1939a) accepts the force of such environmental accounts of transmission. Addressing the claim that there is an "archaic heritage" that passes automatically between generations, he considers the possibility that it is better explained by the biological tendency of each person to react in a similar way to the events of their lives. Freud, however, was not at all satisfied with such explanations, and was convinced that there is inbuilt knowledge of certain events that have occurred in the history of civilisation in general and (in *Moses and Monotheism*, with its focus on the Jews) in the experience of a particular people.

> When we study the reactions to early traumas, we are quite often
> surprised to find that they are not strictly limited to what the subject
> himself has really experienced but diverge from it in a way which fits
> in much better with the model of a phylogenetic event and, in general,
> can only be explained by such an influence. (Freud, 1939a, p. 99)

Freud identifies what he regards as a key reason why the more
obvious explanations of transmission are inadequate: that the reaction
of the individual to a specific set of circumstances very often seems not
to be linked clearly either to the nature of that circumstance or to "what
the subject himself has really experienced". There is also an argument
to *intensity*, in the sense that the degree of attachment to certain behaviours seems to Freud to be inexplicable if one only considers contem-
poraneous events and personal experiences. For Freud, only what is
repressed can return with the force required to ensure neurotic attachment to irrational ideas. Religion relies on this for its sustenance and so
do other unaccountable commitments and madly held positions,
including the most problematic forms of social identity.

It is on the basis of arguments of this kind that Freud feels he
cannot do without the assumption that something is passed down
directly through the generations, unmediated by experience and not
explicable by "direct communication and of the influence of education" (Freud, 1939a, p. 99). His full statement of this demonstrates his
awareness that he is holding to a view that will itself seem irrational
and that is at variance, by the mid-1930s, with the collective view of
evolution held in scientific communities. But never mind, he thinks;
the truth has to be maintained even if no one else sees it that way.

> When I spoke of the survival of a tradition among a people or of the
> formation of a people's character, I had mostly in mind an inherited
> tradition of this kind and not one transmitted by communication. Or
> at least I made no distinction between the two and was not clearly
> aware of my audacity in neglecting to do so. My position, no doubt, is
> made more difficult by the present attitude of biological science,
> which refuses to hear of the inheritance of acquired characters by
> succeeding generations. I must, however, in all modesty confess that
> nevertheless I cannot do without this factor in biological evolution.
> (Freud, 1939a, pp. 99–100)

"In all modesty" means that Freud is confident that his view of evolution is accurate, whatever the scientific evidence might suggest—an

attitude that did not endear him to his many critics. His view of what is passed down is very precise and concrete: the "inherited tradition" to which he refers comprises "not only dispositions but also subject-matter – memory-traces of the experience of earlier generations" (p. 99). In summary (p. 132),

> We must finally make up our minds to adopt the hypothesis that the psychical precipitates of the primaeval period became inherited property which, in each fresh generation, called not for acquisition but only for awakening.

Freud's account of what the detailed content of these archaic memories might be is well known and needs little elaboration here, though it is worth stressing the centrality of the father to the whole story. Briefly, in *Totem and Taboo* (Freud, 1912–1913), he argues that civilisation is set in motion when an original "primal father" who possesses all the women in his "horde", is murdered and then eaten by his sons. Because they felt not only hate for their father, but also love, the murder haunts them and encourages them, out of guilt and remorse, to set up the father as a "totem" and to incorporate his terror within them. As with the development of the individual's superego, what had been an external authority was incorporated internally as a sense of guilt, more powerful and unassailable for all that. In addition, to prevent a repetition of the primal situation, the brothers, under the shadow of the totem, imposed certain rules on themselves to regulate their relations and restrain their passions. "The dead father became stronger than the living one had been", asserts Freud (1912–1913, p. 143). Freud uses this as both a "just-so" story to account for the origins of civilisation and a model for his notions of acquired inheritance: in every generation, the same ambivalence towards the primal father, the same sense of guilty and murderous envy, is present in every human subject. These intergenerational links are insufficiently explained by overt modes of social transmission; rather, there is an inherited disposition to repeat the traumatic original event, triggered into action by some experience in the actual life of the individual concerned. Freud assumes the existence of a mental mechanism that allows each individual access to another's unconscious, and, through this, he assumes that every generation opens up a communicational channel through which the original traumatic killing of the father is passed down. He writes (p. 159),

For psycho-analysis has shown us that everyone possesses in his unconscious mental activity an apparatus which enables him to interpret other people's reactions, that is, to undo the distortions which other people have imposed on the expression of their feelings. An unconscious understanding such as this of all the customs, ceremonies and dogmas left behind by the original relation to the father may have made it possible for later generations to take over their heritage of emotion.

Something unsettling arises from all this. The idea that there might be a way of directly inheriting the outcomes of a primal event is part of the general notion of the possibility of "inheritance of acquired characteristics" known as Lamarckism. Freud's adoption of this view was, for many, an embarrassing slip, though there is also some evidence that this need not be the case if one considers it in its full historical context. For Yerushalmi (1991), the continuity of Jewish identity is attested to by the pervasive Lamarckian assumptions in *Moses and Monotheism* —the idea that specific "learnt" characteristics can be passed down through the generations, so that all Jews share not just a sense of a past history, but the actual memory trace of that history, embodied and internalised, and linking them with one another through a mysterious yet material bond. Yerushalmi might have had his own axe to grind, intent as he was on recovering Freud for Jewish tradition, but the question of how memory operates as an unending sore—how, if one can think of it this way, Jewish inheritance can be *melancholic*—does seem to have exercised Freud avidly. Lamarckism expressively dramatises the complications here, because it both asserts the force of inheritance and contests its irremediability. Slavet (2009) explains how Lamarckism was respectable in the 1920s as a potentially environmental alternative to radical Darwinism. She argues that, at the time Freud was writing *Moses and Monotheism*, the attraction of Lamarckism was that it offered the prospect that changes in social conditions could produce long-lasting alterations in the characteristics of a people, so that the attributes of Jewishness were not necessarily fixed for all time. For this reason, Lamarckism lined up with Jews and Bolsheviks; neo-Darwinism with anti-Semitism and the Nazis. She writes,

> Thus, while Jews were often stereotypically associated with Bolshevism, they were often drawn to it partly by a shared logic of

Lamarckian environmentalism supporting the idea that the inequities
of the present were determined by historical conditions that could and
should be changed in the future. (Slavet, 2009, p. 78)

Things could change, albeit not easily. The adoption of a Lamarckian framework allowed Freud both to emphasise supposedly historical events and a mode of biological or "racial" transmission.
Memories of real occurrences could be passed on from one generation
to another, unconsciously fixing Jewishness as a shared cultural identity not dependent on beliefs or attitudes adopted by any particular
person. Those "dark emotional powers" binding Jews together are
somehow transmitted across the ages, as well as having a tangible
presence between people who otherwise have little to do with one
another. Given the right circumstances—anti-Semitic Europe, for
example—they come to the fore, pressing Jews into identification with
one another and renewing their fantasies and archaic fears.

Despite all this, one has to wonder why Freud argued that
primeval inheritance and Lamarckism was a more satisfying explanation of the transmission of values, identities, and complexes than
would be either a more psychological account of primal fantasy
(shared fantasies that people draw on when dealing with psychic challenges, which in group analytic terms might be coded as expressions
of the social unconscious), or the simpler view that gives pre-
eminence to cultural materials and specific intergenerational identifications. After all, as many authors have shown, Freud himself knew
that important elements of Jewish identity were not automatically
transmitted. Circumcision is the prime instance here: according to
Freud, it is central to male Jewish identity and cultural affinity, yet it
has to be enacted in every single individual instance, for otherwise the
psychic markings of circumcision do not appear (Geller, 2007; Slavet,
2009). Why could Freud not simply have said that each generation
unconsciously passes on its fantasies and fears to the next?

There is too much psychoanalysis of Freud around in the world,
understanding everything about his theory in terms of his personal
foibles and fascinations, but maybe there is room for one more to
bring us back to the question of how transmission occurs. Rose (2007)
argues that the purpose of his Lamarckism was to account for Jewish
identity and that this has to be understood as a personal quest for
Freud, divorced from questions of belief. By the 1930s, she thinks,

Freud has moved from a kind of cultural therapeutics in which psychoanalytic rationalism can conquer social unreason, to a more limited ambition of explaining why and how groups stay together and identity is passed on, "To understand why people, from generation to generation – with no solid ground and in the teeth of the most historically unsympathetic conditions – *hold on*" (p. 83). As Rose hints, there is something very personal in all this. Freud was at pains, at times, to deny his Jewish heritage, or, at least, his knowledge and any residual religious attachment. This left him with little alternative but to assume some kind of automatic transmission of Jewish identity—otherwise, how could he, so secular and atheistic, so ignorant of the Jewish tradition, have felt such a pull? The easy answer that it was due to anti-Semitism was partly true but insufficient to explain the "dark emotional powers" mentioned earlier, so the mystic Lamarckian link was called into play. However, we know that Freud's assertions of ignorance were duplicitous. Yerushalmi (1991) rather persuasively documents evidence suggesting not only that Freud's father remained knowledgeable about, and, at least to some degree, committed to, Judaism throughout his life (tempering Freud's assertion about his "estrangement"), but also that Freud himself retained at least some knowledge of Judaism. Taught religion by the inspirational Samuel Hammerschlag, Freud might have focused on Judaism's ethical principles, but is unlikely never to have come into contact with its forms or its language. Indeed, even though the Freud family "spoke German and ignored such observances as kashrut and the Sabbath", once they had moved to Vienna when Freud was three years old, they still recognised some major Jewish holidays and some scholars claim that Freud would still have heard his father's "adept . . . Hebrew recitation of the Passover service" (Klein, 1985, p. 42).

How can we put together Freud's denial of Jewish knowledge and direct inheritance from his father with the assertion of a general phylogenetic inheritance that is based on the murder of a *primal* father but, in important ways, by-passes the *actual* one? It is not necessary to be a psychoanalyst to know that Freud had an ambivalent relationship with his father, Jacob. He tells us as much in several of the dreams he presents in *The Interpretation of Dreams*, a book that he also explicitly states to be "a portion of my own self-analysis, my reaction to my father's death – that is to say, to the most important event, the most poignant loss, of a man's life" (Freud, 1900a, p. xxvi). Whatever his own abandonment of Hassidism, Jacob Freud clearly invested in his son's Jewish education and maintained a connection with him around Judaism into the 1890s. Yet, Freud was both embarrassed by his father and lived in some anxiety that he had let him down, as well as having a fear of usurping or surpassing him. Perhaps it is not too wild a claim to suggest that the Lamarckian intuition, held by Freud against his own better instincts, or, at least, his scientific knowledge, was a way of relieving himself from the burden of being his father's Jewish son. That is to say, there is a mode of inheritance being claimed here, a way of having a direct link back to Moses, which certainly "explains" the way intense identifications and identity complexes can arise in the most surprising places. However, the simpler model, whereby what is not worked through in one generation becomes a mystery and a task for the next, might actually be harder to acknowledge. It places each of us in personal relationships with our parents and also with the social world in which we live; it is full of messy and unwanted details about other people's lives; it forces us to face up to what we have and have not been given, and what we wanted and what we could never ask for or give back in return. Abstracting this into the far distant past makes it ghostly, which suggests that it should also make it harder to deal with. But this is not actually the case. The immediate, detailed encounter is harder to manage. The ghost that returns is not that of the primal father of prehistory, grabbing the women and slain by the sons. The ghost that haunts is not the lawgiver who cannot be tolerated and has to be destroyed. The ghosts are, for each and every one of us, Freud included, our own parents and intimates, with all of whom we struggle and whose legacy is never fully worked through. We are inhabited by them; that is explanation enough for the toughness and inscrutability of our identifications, the way we keep on with unmanageable material even though we wish we could leave it all untouched, or, at least, leave it all behind.

References

Abraham, N., & Torok, M. (1986). *The Wolf Man's Magic Word: A Cryptonomy*. Minneapolis, MN: University of Minnesota Press.

Abraham, N., & Torok, M. (1994). *The Shell and the Kernel: Renewals of Psychoanalysis*. Chicago, IL: University of Chicago Press.

Derrida, J. (1986). *Fors*: The Anglish words of Nicolas Abraham and Maria Torok. Foreword. In: N. Abraham & M. Torok (Eds.), *The Wolf Man's Magic Word: A Cryptonomy* (pp. xi–iil). Minneapolis, MN: University of Minnesota Press.

Freud, E. (Ed.) (1961). *Letters of Sigmund Freud 1873–1939*. London: Hogarth Press.

Freud, S. (1900a). *The Interpretation of Dreams. S. E.*, 4: ix–627. London: Hogarth.

Freud, S. (1912–1913). *Totem and Taboo. S. E.*, vii–162. London: Hogarth.

Freud, S. (1923b). *The Ego and the Id. S. E.*, 19: 1–66. London: Hogarth.

Freud, S. (1930a). *Civilization and its Discontents. S.E.*, 21: 57–146. London: Hogarth.

Freud, S. (1939a). *Moses and Monotheism. S. E.*, 23: 1–138. London: Hogarth.

Geller, J. (2007). *On Freud's Jewish Body: Mitigating Circumcisions*. New York: Fordham University Press.

Gouri, H. (1960). Heritage. In: T. Carmi (Ed.), *The Penguin Book of Hebrew Verse* (p. 565). Harmondsworth: Penguin, 1981.

Grinberg, L., & Grinberg, R. (1974). The problem of identity and the psychoanalytical process. *International Review of Psychoanalysis*, 1: 499–507.

Hopper, E. (2003). *The Social Unconscious: Selected Papers*. London: Jessica Kingsley.

Klein, D. (1985). *Jewish Origins of the Psychoanalytic Movement*. Chicago, IL: University of Chicago Press.

Rose, J. (2007). *The Last Resistance*. London: Verso.

Slavet, E. (2009). *Racial Fever: Freud and the Jewish Question*. New York: Fordham.

Spiegel, S. (1967). *The Last Trial*. Woodstock: Jewish Lights Publishing, 1993.

Volkan, V. (2002). *The Third Reich in the Unconscious*. New York: Brunner-Routledge.

Yerushalmi, Y. (1991). *Freud's Moses*. New Haven, CT: Yale University Press.

Zornberg, A. (2009). *The Murmuring Deep: Reflections on the Biblical Unconscious*. New York: Schocken.

CHAPTER TWO

Further thoughts about the foundation matrix, the social unconscious, and the collective unconscious: the myth of the Tower of Babel

Hanni Biran

Introduction

In this chapter, I try to integrate some of Foulkes' ideas regarding what he called the "foundation matrix" with some of Bion's ideas about what he called "group mentality", "group culture", and "cultural myths". I will focus on the study of myths and unconscious patterns of communication.

Foulkes argues that

> . . . even a group of total strangers, being of the same species and more narrowly of the same culture, share a fundamental mental matrix. To this their closer acquaintance and their intimate exchanges add consistently so that they form a current, ever moving and ever developing dynamic matrix. (Foulkes, 1990, p. 228)

His idea of "the fundamental mental matrix" is crucial for us as group analysts. We tend to forget the powerful influence of the contextual society on our small groups. We also tend to share an illusion that our analytic room exists in a kind of empty space, whereas, in fact, the foundation matrix always envelopes and intertwines with the dynamic matrix of the group.

Three concepts of Bion resonate with the concept of the foundation matrix: the first is the concept of group mentality:

> ... the pool to which the anonymous contributions are made, and through which the impulses and desires implicit in these contributions are gratified. Any contribution to this group mentality must enlist the support of, or be in conformity with, the other anonymous contributions of the group. I should expect the group mentality to be distinguished by a uniformity that contrasted with the diversity of thought in the mentality of the individuals who have contributed to its formation. (Bion, 1961, p. 50)

The second concept is "group culture": "... those aspects of the behaviour of the group which seemed to be born of the conflict between group mentality and the desires of the individual" (Bion, 1961, p. 59).

The anonymous "contributions", "the uniformity", "the pool", and "the group culture" all develop in hidden and silent ways. They are connected to the foundation matrix because they build the common infrastructure of society. They tell us about the social environment, the values and beliefs of group members as well as about their language.

The third concept of Bion is the "cultural myth" (Bion, 1962, p. 79). The main myths that interest Bion are the Tower of Babel (Bion, 1963, p. 46), the eating from the Tree of Knowledge (Bion, 1963, p. 92) and Oedipus the King (Bion, 1967, p. 86). Cultural myths are elements of the foundation matrix. Myths are in the infrastructure of society at large. Bion thinks that these myths repeat generation after generation and are essential to the basic culture of humanity, and, therefore, they are universal, and not particular to any one society.

These concepts of Foulkes and Bion pertain to the study of the social unconscious (Hopper, 2003a; Hopper & Weinberg, 2011). However, they also pertain to the study of the collective unconscious conceptualised by Jung, who described an impersonal layer in the psyche, which he called the collective unconscious, as a priori given, containing universal patterns and forces. These archetypes have a numinous quality, suggesting that the species is rooted in the mind of God (Hopper & Weinberg, 2011; Noack, 2011). When we explore the myth of Babel, we find that the timeless, ancient, and universal roots of the collective unconscious, as well as variations of it, manifest in the social unconscious of each society, and the foundation matrix of it.

To summarise: the main concepts that I will explore belong to different theories: the foundation matrix of Foulkes, the cultural myth of Bion, the collective unconscious of Jung, and the social unconscious of Hopper. However, despite their differences, there is a profound connection among them. They pertain to societal processes of which people are unconscious. They are like messages from the past that enacted in the present and have intense influence on the future.

I shall now focus on Bion's theory for analysing the myth of the Tower of Babel.

Myths as essential for culture

Bion regarded myths as important representations of the key components of culture and as important elements of culture. His view is similar to that of Levi Strauss (Boon & Schneider, 1974), who describes the similarity among myths of different cultures:

> On the one hand it would seem that in the course of a myth anything is likely to happen. But on the other hand, this apparent arbitrariness is belied by the astounding similarity between myths collected in widely different regions. Therefore, the problem: If the content of myth is contingent [i.e., arbitrary], how are we to explain the fact that myths throughout the world are so similar?

Lévi-Strauss proposed that universal laws must govern mythical thought and resolve this seeming paradox, producing similar myths in different cultures. Each myth may seem unique, but he proposed it is just one particular instance of a universal law of human thought. In studying myth, Lévi-Strauss tries "to reduce apparently arbitrary data to some kind of order, and to attain a level at which a kind of necessity becomes apparent, underlying the illusions of liberty" (Boon & Schneider, 1974, p. 802).

Foulkes and Bion are concerned with the immanent tension between the life of persons and the life of their societies. Foulkes thinks in terms of the gestalt of an observer's perceptions, that is, figure/ground (Foulkes, 2002, p. 131), and Bion thinks in terms of what he calls "binocular vision" (Bion, 1961, p. 8). However, Bion also believes that myth simultaneously expresses both the life story of the individual person and the life of culture and society. He also referred to myth in his relentless search concerning the constitutive elements of psychoanalysis. In his clinical practice, he often discovered that his patients had omnipotent fantasies, and he tried to find the roots of these fantasies within both the social unconscious and the collective unconscious, although he did not use these two terms. To some extent, Bion thought that the study of myths might provide further insight into the roots of omnipotent fantasies. Especially important was that myths included what he called "emotional knowledge". It can be argued that, in contrast to Bion's perspective on this matter, Foulkes' thinking developed more along the lines of individuals having certain tendencies to personify roles that are implied in particular myths, or, as Bion would have put it, they have a valence for taking certain roles. Foulkes also argued that it is a matter of the gestalt of the observer's perception as to whether a particular myth is an element in the culture or an element in the personality of the person who is personifying a particular process or enacting the unconscious constraints of a role in the myth.

Bion believed that myth evolves from the *alpha function* (Bion, 1967) and shares some elements with dream thinking. The dream, indeed, is one reflection of the individual's private myth. According to Bion, those who "wrote" myths actually succeeded in conveying their personal dream in a way that communicates to and is relevant to every other human being. The mythographer has the characteristics of the genius: she has the ability to translate her own inner experience into a narrative that speaks to the whole of humanity.

Myth is a universal story. However, the contents and structure of a myth may vary from culture to culture and/or society to society. There are many variations on the underlying basic structure, but they all deal with human drives, human morality, and with human limitations compared to the omnipotence of God. This basic similarity points to the universality of the human "mind".

Bion also describes myths in terms of a mathematical equation with one variable, or unknown element. This unknown component has the function of introducing new material into the myth across the generations. The implication is that myths come with variations, and that there are as yet unknown myths (or variations of old ones) that will manifest themselves only in the future. These future myths will construct some variations of the older myths.

Since they express drive and emotion by means of imagery, myths are a type of innate preconception. It is on the basis of this type of imagery that we can construct the concepts that form the basis of psychoanalysis. For Bion, the four great elemental and universal myths of Adam and Eve's eating from the Tree of Knowledge, the Tower of Babel, the story of Oedipus Rex, and the story of Narcissus repeat themselves throughout the generations, both in the cultures of all societies and in the personal life of each individual member of them.

I shall now consider some of the relationships between myth and the psychic life of individuals.

Myths and psychoanalysis

In his *Elements of Psychoanalysis*, Bion (1963) argues that the myths of the Tree of Knowledge, the Tower of Babel and of Oedipus Rex have similar core elements: the desire to know and to penetrate the riddle of life, and the attempt to attain divine, omniscient knowledge. This arrogance is called "the sin of hubris". In these narratives, man is confronted with his limitations. He is punished for his curiosity, but this punishment brings about growth. The paradox, traditionally called "the Fortunate Fall", is that man wants to know, meets with pain, exile, a fall—but it is exactly due to these crises that new growth occurs, leading to a condition that is fuller and deeper than before. Every patient, Bion believed, tells something about her life in terms of these myths. Every person has the experience of disillusion, when, momentarily, she feels exiled from Paradise. Every person sometimes feels not understood, misunderstood, and unable to communicate. We each have moments when we do not find any common language with others in our group. We are all born to parents and go through the oedipal conflict. The issue of narcissism also preoccupies us all, at one time or another: how much of ourselves can we dedicate to ourselves and how much should we address to those around us?

So, similar themes appear in the specific biographies of all patients. Hence, we must attend to each patient's story as to an equation with an unknown element. While the fixed elements recur, their permutations are infinite. If we want to find out about the patient's own psychic make-up, according to Bion, we must look in the patient's narrative for the specific connections among these components. Bion writes about the analogy that, just as combinations of the various letters of the alphabet give rise to different words, psychic elements are grouped in various, unique sequences. Every patient comes with his life mystery that the therapist can decipher by tracing the connections among his psychic components. When these connections, through misreading and misinterpretation, are inappropriate, a monstrous psychological reality might arise: Bion's example here is the story of the monstrous sphinx who incorporates links between elements that cannot actually be linked. The patient's riddle is interpreted through the work of psychoanalysis, which acknowledges a priori that some parts will never be exposed. In Bion's language, such parts are buried, either in the past, in the zone of forgetfulness, or in the future, inside the thoughts that we shall never dare to think. There is a danger that a patient and an analyst can create a monstrous interpretation and this can haunt the analysis for a very long time. When the analysis is based on bad feeding and bad digestion, it can happen in group analysis as well. It is the task of the group analyst to discover the bad dynamic matrix and to free the group and himself of the bad collaboration. However, while Bion was dealing with those aspects of myth that are relevant to the individual psyche, he was also interested in the social, group-related side of myth.

His analysis of the Tower of Babel episode exemplifies how myth articulates the relationship between individual and society.

The seventh servant and the container

When we look at the story of Babel, Bion's notion of *common sense* (CS) (Bion, 1965, p. 2) can be very useful. Common sense refers to the way in which a number of senses come together and jointly create another sense. Here, the senses mutually support each other for the sake of interpreting the information. According to Bion, this type of collaboration enables us to gain insights and draw conclusions. Bion then establishes intuition on this interconnection among the senses, their parallel activation along channels that cross and give rise to a unified experience. Fundamentally, in fact, intuition is another word for common sense. For Bion (1965, p. 18), intuition has a crucial role in how both the verbal and the non-verbal communications are processed in the course of the analytic session.

Still, because he was aware that intuition is a sixth sense, constituted from a combination of the other five senses, it has an indefin-
able, unfathomable quality. An intuitive interpretation, therefore, will
always leave room for doubt. There will always be a certain surplus
of unknown elements that remain inaccessible to intuitive interpretation. Here, Bion offers a paraphrase to Kipling's children's poem, "Six
Servants". In this poem, the six servants represent the questions asked
by the child who is discovering the world: Who? What? When?
Where? How? Why? They are the questions of the curious person who
learns from experience. To this, Bion adds a seventh servant, which is
the question that knows not how to be asked. This question is like the
missing piece of the puzzle. It is the unsolvable riddle of life. The
missing piece of the puzzle resonates with Bion's Indian childhood
that was seen by him as a very mysterious and incomprehensible
period of his life. This idea echoes the four questions asked at the
Jewish Passover by the youngest child present. In the same text there
is one son that "does not know how to ask". The same kind of puzzle
exists in Freud's comment about the universality of a black spot at the
heart of every dream that seems to be unknowable, and, in Bion, the
concept of Becoming O.

In Chapter Twenty-seven of his *Learning from Experience* (1962),
Bion argues that no psychoanalysis can occur where both therapist
and patient do not have the ability to tolerate doubt. We must take this
ability as a sine qua non of the analytic process. The correlation
between the senses serves mainly to illustrate the therapist's ability to
co-ordinate among the various emotions she experiences vis-à-vis the
patient. Here, it is important to remember that when Bion refers to the
ability to see, he always also means *emotional vision*. For instance, the
therapist may feel love for his patient and, in another context, hate
him. Yet, inside herself, the therapist preserves a whole image, knowing that her love and hate were directed at the same person who was
manifesting different sides of her personality.

The various feelings that coexist within the therapist actually
constitute a type of containment. Acting as a type of "sleeve", as Bion
calls them, these emotions absorb the patient's material. While the
therapist will each time respond from a different sleeve, the container
in which all these sleeves are united stays whole and permanent,
enclosing a whole picture. The different emotions are channels of
communication via which the therapist is able to know her patient

better and, at the same time, also become more familiar with herself. If these channels are to be open simultaneously, intuition needs to work, because I believe that it is intuition that is responsible, during the session, when a whole crowd of feelings emerges, for the ongoing functioning of containment. It seems to me that containment is a function that is maintained by intuition. While it keeps the various emotional channels open, it sustains doubt at the same time. All the above concepts: the ability to tolerate doubt, the sleeves of containment, emotional vision, common sense, intuition, all put together are central for Bion's thinking and they are the components of his theory about knowing and not knowing as the main position of the psychoanalyst.

Bion argued that common sense also emerges from another type of collaboration. This occurs when a number of people who have the same response to a shared emotional experience can connect with the group and the society, and shift from myth as an expression of the psychic life of persons to its expression in the culture. When Antigone buries her brother against Creon's orders, a type of intuitive social agreement occurs about the justness of Antigone's action—the dead body should be buried. Over and beyond the king's decree, there is an ethics, a sort of natural justice, to which all human beings subscribe. The group is built on intuitive, unspoken, and sometimes even unconscious, agreements. Group belonging relies on the individual's ability to emotionally communicate with her group and to experience herself as part of, and in agreement with, the group. We may argue that it is "common" sense that allows us to maintain our connection to other people. When they are in agreement with each other, group members confirm each other and, as a result, joint knowledge comes into existence. Group members communicate, personal knowledge transforms into common, public knowledge.

The link between egocentric and sociocentric aspects

Yet, every person is also, and at the same time, a narcissistic creature. Positive narcissism is what enables the individual in the group to stick to his uniqueness and difference. Individuals must be in touch with groups so that they may grow as a result, but they must be able to preserve the boundaries of self while doing so. The idea of positive narcissism is similar to Kohut's concept of mature narcissism when a person accomplishes his ambitions and ideals.

Much like many other elements in Bion's theory, the common sense occurs in the space of the *link*. In our case, the link in question is that between the egocentric aspect and the sociocentric aspect. The space in which occurs, simultaneously, the difference among group members as well as their agreement and unity is a dynamic space which is crucial for growth, both individual and social. These two elements are mutually enhancing when they connect through a plus-type link.

In the myth of the Tower of Babel these links are destroyed. In *Cogitations*, Bion (1992) shows how the myth of the Tower of Babel inspired him to develop the notion of the *attack on linking*. The link between individual and group may come under attack from different directions.

The individual cannot tolerate the social space and responds with developing a kind of megalomaniac narcissism. He believes he can live without the group, that, in fact, he is much bigger and stronger than it. This breaks the reciprocity between him and the group. As a result, the individual falls prey to grandiose thinking and psychosis. It is similar to a narcissistic personality disorder, but here the emphasis is on the social meaning.

Another situation in which the individual might sever his relations with the group is when, following trauma in the social sphere, he withdraws into himself, gives up on society as a source of support, and emotionally disconnects from the group. This is the basis of what Hopper (2003b), in his theory of a fourth basic assumption of Incohesion, terms *aggregation,* and Gordon Lawrence and co-writers (1996) term *me-ness,* that is, when a person relies on himself exclusively. In these circumstances, the linking of the individual to the group is under attack.

The group fails to tolerate its own multiplicity and denies the differences between people, erases personal characteristics, invades the boundaries of the self and transforms the members of the group into one undifferentiated mass. This is what Hopper calls, in contradistinction to aggregation, *massification* , through which the group generates a grandiose, merged position in which the members of it lose their individuality. Belonging to the group gives them a sense of omnipotence. In contrast with the previous case, here the linking of the group to the individual comes under attack. Now, it is the group that runs the danger of becoming immersed in a social psychosis.

Bion's conceptualisation of three basic assumptions and Hopper's conceptualisation of a fourth basic assumption are relevant to the study of societies. For example, totalitarian societies have been always based on dependency, and fight/flight, as well as on massification as a defence against aggregation. Religious establishments have been always based on dependency, pairing, and massification. People come to listen to an enthusiastic preacher, to sing and to pray together. Many communities follow the study of Kabbala or even the study of Scientology. Gurus are paired unconsciously with God. In Israel, the right wing, mainly in the settlements in Judea and Samaria, is based on the massification pole of Incohesion. The settlers feel united with the one and absolute truth that they have to conquer the Holy Land. However, the left wing is weak and divided and the emotions are in the aggregation pole of Incohesion. These phenomena are properties of the foundation matrix of Israel.

We can, therefore, say that the linking between the individual and the group requires that both individual and the group know their limits. While the group should provide the soil in which its member individuals can grow, these individuals must acknowledge that it is, indeed, this soil that allows them to grow. However, grandiose, omnipotent, and megalomaniac phenomena will appear, both in the individual and in the group, when these links are attacked. This idea resonates with Kaes' theory that the individual is inextricably bound up with the narcissistic needs and fears of others. Subjectivity means being the subject of a group, woven into the fabric of intersubjective relations (Kirshner, 2006).

The Tower of Babel: the monolithic group as a hero

Although it is short and condensed, which is typical of many biblical episodes, the Tower of Babel narrative touches us profoundly. Unique among myths, this story has no hero at its centre. Instead, it features a group that obliterates individual differences, to the point of even discarding the position of the leader. In this group, all members have become anonymous in order to rally to the overarching, grandiose project: to vie with divine knowledge. In the words of the Bible, Genesis 11, 1–9:

> And the whole earth was of one language, and of one speech. And it came to pass, as they journeyed from the east, that they found a plain in the land of Shinar; and they dwelt there. And they said to one another, Go to, let us make brick, and burn them thoroughly. And they had brick for stone, and slime had they for mortar. And they said, Go to, let us build a city and a tower, whose top may reach unto heaven, lest we be scattered abroad upon the face of the whole earth. And the Lord came down to see the city and the tower, which the children of men builded. And the Lord said, Behold, the people is one, and they have all one language; and this they begin to do: and now nothing will be restrained from them, which they have imagined to do. Go to, let us go down, and there confound their language, that they may not understand one another's speech. So the Lord scattered them abroad from thence upon the face of all the earth: and they left off to build the city. Therefore is the name of it called Babel; because the Lord did there confound the language of all the earth: and from thence did the Lord scatter them abroad upon the face of all the earth.

Bion considers the tower as a phallic symbol expressing a megalomaniac wish to compete with God for omniscience. The construction work, using only one type of building material, is unitary, linear and monochrome. "Heaven" is a kind of symbol for mother's body, her "breast" in particular, and her mind (Hopper, 2012a). Language is first of all the mother tongue, and the group wants one collective name and language. The tower represents a great mass that attacks the space where the differences within the group are linked. Difference is annulled in order to boost the omnipotent yearnings of the group. However, when the group comes together around one aim and at one place, it disobeys God's injunction to "Be fruitful and multiply and replenish the earth" (Genesis 2: 28). In their yearning for complete wholeness, the people of Babel try to reach all the way up to divine knowledge. The phallic tower and the omnipotent wishes, according to Bion, are core features of psychoanalysis. The construction of the tower, for him, represents a link of type $-K$. Where doubt is absent, where there is no question, there is no dialogue and the space for growth becomes obstructed. A tower arises, but on flawed foundations. It will, therefore, not be feasible over time.

The omnipotent person is monolithic and she has no questions. Hence, her growth will lose its vitality and impetus, and become bland and drained of colour. Size alone will not make up for the attack on linking. In this uniform and claustrophobic structure, the links among the differences in the group have ceased to exist.

God's punishment of the people of Babel, in Bion's view, is actually a form of reparation. He destroys the tower in order to expose difference, so that what appears as destruction turns out to be growth and what seems to be catastrophic is, in fact, only catastrophic change. This change will bring a flourishing of languages and cultures, and with it a renewed balance between the individual and the group. The idea of the tower effaces difference and replaces it with a fantasy of infinite power. God makes man start anew, to create languages and cultures that will allow the link between man and group. This is where a transformation to +K occurs, entailing the recognition of limitations, of a reality that is not total. This punishment, we could argue, leads to a variety of possible ways to acknowledge limitation. This structure was flawed because it denied difference, doubt, and questions.

In Bion's analysis, the relationship between the depressive and the schizo-paranoid positions works in both directions, where each situation may augment the other: while the depressive position represents the whole and the integrated, the schizo-paranoid position implies the ability to tolerate rupture and fragmentation. In these terms, the Babel narrative is an interesting example of what happens when the schizo-paranoid position amplifies the depressive position. The tower suggests a false degree of integration and wholeness. Once this project was abandoned there was, again, room for growth, and for what Bion called the *positive split*. What this suggests is that each of the dispersed groups, or sub groups, could then acknowledge its limitations and partiality, as well as the existence of other groups with different cultures. The transition to +K occurs when the individual surrenders her claim to the absolute, divine knowledge which she will never attain.

Common non-sense

The Babel episode, for Bion, epitomises a situation in which common sense is replaced by *common non-sense*. When this happens, the human intuition that also acknowledges what is absent vanishes. Fantasy, in such conditions, may come to appear as reality. Thus, the tower is constructed on the grandiose assumption that its "top may reach unto heaven", utterly failing to acknowledge that "heaven" is infinite, and, in this sense, by definition beyond reach and taboo, and, in this sense, by definition subject to punishment. So, the people of Babel have acted on common non-sense and, indeed, the result is that all linking among the people is attacked. Thus, from one extreme, they find themselves at the other: from a state of absolute unity and the total eradication of difference, they now cannot communicate and their words come across as non-sense.

This myth has many implications for the therapeutic discourse. Indeed, the question of language in the therapeutic session greatly preoccupied Bion. He abhorred the barren language of jargon and cliché. How can we connect without becoming caught in a conceptual homogeneity that is impervious to criticism? And how, on the other hand, can therapist and patient achieve an emotionally meaningful level of communication and avoid non-sense?

In his article "Caesura" Bion (1989), following Churchill, mentions how it is often said that the English and the Americans have everything in common except language. While they use the same words, they actually refer to different things, because, of course, language is context and culture dependent. Similarly, Bion argues that although analyst and analysand speak the same language, they do so from different points of departure, and, hence, each might be talking about different things. He likens this to how we can look at a mountain from different angles: what we see is the same mountain, yet being placed in different positions in relation to it we necessarily have different experiences. Bion thinks we should pay attention to this type of disparity in language: it is up to the therapist to cope. Bion suggests that the therapist should use all his senses, pick up the hints, including non-verbal ones, that the patient produces in the here and now, in order to give a fresh interpretation which is based not only on the therapist's viewpoint but also relies on a type of linking with the patient's position. The emotional language is free of jargon and is open to many options, which are impossible when one is caught within a language structure and vocabulary in which words become "things". This is the essence of "fundamentalism", and many clinicians are theoretical fundamentalists in the way they present material and offer interpretation (Hopper, 2003b; 2012b).

Late in his life, in 1977, Bion gave a series of seminars in Rome (Bion, 2005; p. 1). This is how he opened the first of these seminars: "First, I must apologise for not being able to speak Italian, but I am consoled by the thought that the subject I want to discuss is one which I find very difficult to talk about in any language . . ." Later that week, he went as far as suggesting that his inability to speak Italian might even be an advantage: the fact that all other seminar participants did speak Italian might actually be blocking their active search for the language of the unconscious.

In the course of this event in Rome, Bion also said that when the analyst comes to write his case study he should not write what he thinks the analysand has been saying. What Bion recommends is that, after writing his text, the analyst should read it and take out the words we always tend to use in analysis, to go back again and remove even more, until what is left is one sentence that is as short and exact as possible. Apparently, Bion believed it was hard to reach patients via psychoanalytical terminology—instead we must always aim for the language of the unconscious, which is elusive and hard to interpret.

If the therapist makes a constant effort to express clearly and exactly what he thinks and feels at any given moment, the patient may, gradually, come to understand the therapist's language. We must, argues Bion, keep honing and elaborating our therapeutic vocabulary. At the same time, he reminds us that, since communication is not just verbal, we must mobilise our senses so as to extract the non-verbal meanings that arise in the clinic.

Social implications: language and subculture

Bion's work on the links between various types of languages also carries wider social implications. On that level, we see that the encounter between cultures and languages is often accompanied by experiences of pain, inferiority, and humiliation. In Israel, for instance, there is a long history of failures in creating a dialogue with newcomers. The cultural codes of Russian or Ethiopian immigrants are unlike those of native Israelis. These populations tend to be socially marginalised—they continue to live within their own communities. The same process occurs between Israel's Jewish and Arab populations, and between religious and secular Jews. These situations might be based on reconstructions of sibling rivalry at the societal level. In addition, what is behind all this is a fear of the other and a sense that any attempt to connect will result in incomprehensible, chaotic babble or the fragmentation of the mother tongue.

However, what really causes the problem is not language as such, but the associated culture of which it is an element. Holocaust survivors received a cold shoulder and an arrogant reception from Israelis in the 1950s. They were considered no good, incompetents who had somehow survived. Once in Israel, they were branded "sheep who went to the slaughter" and stood for everything that was *not* associated with the born and bred Israeli. The Eichmann trial, in 1961, which provided a stage for survivors' stories, changed this attitude. Yael Moore (2009), a Tel Aviv psychologist who works with Holocaust survivors, says that the most traumatic event of the twentieth century became a collective event in Israel. Translated into Bion's terms, the group became anonymous; it was silenced and the subjectivity of its members was erased. It took a long time for this mood to change. Meanwhile, the great Diaspora heritage was lost. This, in Bion's terms, was a typical attack on linking. Because the survivors were treated as one nameless mass, their specific personal, subjective stories sank into oblivion, a shivering reflection of their being only "numbers" engraved on their arms proclaiming that they are not human beings, but only a kind of product. When, at a later stage, it became possible to articulate the personal narratives, the emotional links needed for the subjectivisation of the survivors came into play.

Jewish people who immigrated to Israel from countries in the Arab world, and whose mother tongue was Arabic, a language with low social and cultural prestige, also knew the pain of languages that do not link. They suffered from a sense of inferiority and shame. It took years until their cultures became interconnected with Israeli–Ashkenazi culture. The change, again, involved a shift in the dominant Ashkenazis' attitude from treating the Sephardi Jews as a homogenous, faceless mass to being able to perceive difference and subjectivity. What was lost, nevertheless, again, was a whole diasporic heritage. The Israeli notion of "melting pot"—a latter day version of the Tower of Babel—epitomises the nation-building effort to turn an entire society into one unified mass, the yearning to erase difference and speak one language. Such a concept of society surrenders the belief in an integrative society whose constitutive parts continue existing in their distinctiveness.

Social dreaming

Charlotte Beradt, in *The Third Reich of Dreams* (1985), documents dreams dreamt in Nazi Germany. She collected dreams, from both Jewish and non-Jewish Germans, that occurred between 1933 and 1939. Keeping in mind what Bion said about the proximity of dream and myth, it is interesting to note that these dreams give visual form to what was about to happen. I shall refer to three dreams, told by Jewish people.

> 1. A Jewish lawyer who lived in Berlin dreamt that he was perceived to have contributed to Germany during the First World War, so he was allowed to continue working as a lawyer in spite of the racial laws. This is what he dreamt in 1935: "I had gone to a concert and had a reserved seat, or at least I thought I had one. However it turned out that my ticket was only an advertisement, and someone else was sitting in my seat. Many other people were in the same situation. With heads bowed, we all slowly left the concert hall by the centre aisle, while the orchestra began playing, 'we have no abiding home here'". (p. 133)

> 2. Another Jewish lawyer, aged 55, was forbidden to continue practicing. He dreamt: "I went to the Ministry of Justice, dressed in my best. The Minister was sitting, surrounded by SS guards, at a huge desk (just like the one seen on photographs of Hitler) and was wearing a cross between a black uniform and a lawyer's robe (this dream must have been caused by the fact that I had been forced to throw away my lawyer's robe the day before). I told the Minister "I charge that the ground is being pulled out from under me". The guards grabbed me and threw me to the floor. Lying there, I said "I even kiss the ground on which you throw me" (p. 134).

> 3. Yet another Jewish lawyer, prominent and successful, had the following dream in 1935: "Two benches were standing side by side in Tiergarten Park, one painted the usual green and the other yellow (in those days, Jews were permitted to sit only on specially painted yellow benches). There was a trash can between them. I sat down on the trash can and hung a sign around my neck like the ones blind beggars sometimes wear—also like those the government makes 'race violators' wear. It read: "*I Make Room for Trash If Need Be*". (p. 135)

Moore says that some of the survivors, mainly those who were in concentration camps, stopped having dreams altogether. Here, the dream froze, became static, and turned into a nightmare. They no longer told a story; myth was destroyed. While the myth of Babel suggests the outcome of "growth", the Holocaust trauma put an end to people's ability to dream and, thus, to achieve symbolisation and concept construction. In the nightmare, the trauma was perpetually iterated. In so far as the nightmare, being a "thing in itself", resembles the Beta element, it leaves no room for the existence of preconception. As the Holocaust terminated dreams as well as myth, its horrors deprived human beings of worth, reducing them, instead, into statistical data, objects stripped of their subjectivity. Masses of people were put to death using industrial methods. Nazi society strangled all myths except one: the supremacy of the one race all of whose members must be exact copies of one perfect model. So we can see Nazi ideology as a modern and radical variant of the myth of Babel. It is a consummate instance of grandiose wishes that eventually crash. As we can see from what happened in the Holocaust, dreams and myths are a sine qua non for growth and for the preservation of humans' emotional life.

These dreams also illustrate that these people were deeply aware of the regime's totalitarianism and "foretold" what was about to happen. Their dreams articulate the anticipated future of the society. Straddling the personal and the public, they share some components with myth. According to Gordon Lawrence, such dreams connect and demonstrate parts of the foundation matrix. Lawrence's decision to call his social dream-telling a "matrix" is not incidental, but is a continuation of Foulkes' "foundation matrix".

Derrida's Towers of Babel

In her introduction to the Hebrew translation of Derrida's *Des Tours de Babel* (1990), Michal Ben Naftali argues that for myths to continue arising and for growth to go on happening, we need an open space. Such space is obstructed by monolithic, fully completed towers. Similarly, I have argued above how, in a fascist society that insists on a uniform truth, indeed, the space of thinking becomes clogged and nothing new grows. According to Michal Ben Naftali, towers must stay suspended in mid-air, always at risk of collapse: this is what ensures us a history, what gives us air to breathe and allows us to go on building. No stone that cannot be turned. In the interval between the tower and its collapse, says Ben Naftali, the agony of Babel occurs.

Derrida, in *Des Tours de Babel*, mentions a certain *disorder* that is reflected in an inability to complete something that is part of the construction work, of the architecture. Thanks to this type of positive disorder, the tower does not become too homogenous and complete. It is the plurality of tongues that reins in the dominant tendencies of system and cohesion. Thus, a kind of internal constraint to formalisation arises as a result of the fact that the construction work is left unfinished. The system deconstructs itself, then to be reconstructed in a different way. It is fascinating to observe these meeting points between Derrida's deconstruction and Bion's notion of catastrophic change. Catastrophic change throws the existing order into disarray, preventing it from going on and building up, but, as the present structure is shattered, change becomes possible. A new space for growth opens up.

The 2006 film *Babel*, by Mexican filmmaker Alejandro Gonzalez Inarritu, depicts a postmodern attempt at erecting a Tower of Babel. Inarritu's film bears out Bion's claim that the myth of Babel reappears in various guises. A visitor from Japan gives his friend, a villager from Morocco, a gun without realising that the weapon might fall into the wrong hands. The gun actually ends up with some children who mistake it for a toy. Being shot at inadvertently by one of the children, Europeans who are visiting a quiet and friendly Moroccan village become convinced that the villagers are terrorists: the tourists flee in a panic, leaving behind their American friend, whose wife has accidentally been injured by the gun with which the children were playing. The US police, when they face Mexicans, react with arrogance and a total lack of interest. They neither look at the person nor listen to her or his story. Thus, entire chains of communication become badly tangled and tragedy strikes. The illusion that one culture can come to be totally fluent in the codes of another culture is shattered. Here, several cultures meet: American, Mexican, Moroccan, and Japanese. On the face of it, communication seems to be smooth. With a smattering of English, it seems, you can cope everywhere. The world, in an age of globalisation and communication, has indeed been reduced to a global village. It is easy to travel anywhere. However, the film illustrates how technology fails to register the profound differences between cultures and so the attempt to create unity leads to a severe attack on linking. In fact, each culture addresses the other from within its own terms, oblivious to the others' cultural codes. The bid to ignore difference increases the linguistic cacophony, and, therefore, misunderstanding, leading to alienation and fear.

Conclusion

The social space, a subject Bion addressed frequently, should shield singularity and difference and safeguard the boundaries of each culture and individuals within it. At the very same time, though, a continuous effort must be made to learn about, and communicate with, other cultures and other individuals, with the aim of growth and avoiding an attack on linking. This idea is similar to the positive aspect of Hopper's massification in oscillation with aggregation. There are some turning points from aggregation to massification and *vice versa* which are optimal. Aggregation allows for the emergence of individuality, and massification enables the survival of the group. We can feel these two opposite movements inside Bion's concept of catastrophic change. Catastrophic change (Bion, 1967) is the core of the myth of the tower of Babel.

A foundation matrix contains the similarities and, at the same time, the endless variations of the myth. The concept of the foundation matrix enables us to look at the birth and history of myths. In this chapter, I tried to analyse the myth of Babel as an interesting illustration of myths within a foundation matrix. I chose this myth because it deals with issues of language. In our professional field, there are many different jargons for the exploration of the individual and the social unconscious as well as the collective unconscious, which are three sets of aspects of the same phenomenon. The foundation matrix helps us to discover the common roots of thinking and, at the same time, to search for links and for ways of communication among different points of view and frames of reference.

This chapter is based on an integration of several theories. All of them deal with the internal and the external world. All of them agree that there are issues which one person cannot contain and he needs a group of people to share his emotions, ideas, fears, and so on. When we explore culture and social structures, we find out that there are elements which the small group cannot contain and it needs society at large for understanding the complexity of myths, of the foundation matrix, of the collective unconscious, and of the social unconscious. This exploration is dynamic and never ending, because societies are always in a process of changing.

References

Beradt, C. (1985). *The Third Reich of Dreams*. Wellingborough, Northamptonshire: Aquarian Press.

Bion, W. R. (1961). *Experiences in Groups and Other Papers*. London: Tavistock.

Bion, W. R. (1962). *Learning From Experience*. London: Maresfield Reprints.

Bion, W. R. (1963). *Elements of Psychoanalysis*. London: Maresfield Reprints.

Bion, W. R. (1965). *Transformation*. London: Maresfield Reprints.

Bion, W. R. (1967). *Second Thoughts*. London: Maresfield Reprints.

Bion, W. R. (1989). Caesura. In: *Two Papers: The Grid and The Caesura* (pp. 35–56). London: Karnac.

Bion, W. R. (1992). *Cogitations*. London: Karnac.

Bion, W. R. (2005). *The Italian Seminars*. London: Karnac.

Boon, J., & Schneider, D. (1974). Kinship vis-à-vis myth contrasts in Levi Strauss Approaches to Cross Cultural Comparison. *American Anthropologist, New Series, 76*(4): 799–817.

Derrida, J. (1990). Des Tours de Babel. In: *Psyche* (pp. 191–225). Paris: Ed Galilee.

Foulkes, S. H. (1990). The group as a matrix of the individual's mental life. In: *Selected Papers* (pp. 223–233). London: Karnac.

Foulkes, S. H. (2002). *Group Analytic Psychotherapy, Method and Principles*. London: Karnac.

Hopper, E. (2003a). *The Social Unconscious: Selected Papers*. London: Jessica Kingsley.

Hopper, E. (2003b). *Traumatic Experience in the Unconscious Life of Groups: The Fourth Basic Assumption: Incohesion: Aggregation/Massification or (ba) I:A/M*. London: Jessica Kingsley.

Hopper, E. (2012a). Personal communication.

Hopper, E. (Ed.) (2012b). Introduction. In: *Trauma and Organisations*. London: Karnac.

Hopper E., & Weinberg, H. (Eds.) (2011). Introduction. In: *The Social Unconscious in Persons, Groups and Societies: Volume 1: Mainly Theory*. London: Karnac.

Kirshner, L. A. (2006). The work of Rene Kaes: intersubjective transmission in families, groups and culture. *Journal of the American Psychoanalytic Association, 54*: 1005–1013.

Lawrence, W. G., Bain, A., & Gould, L. J. (1996). The fifth basic assumption. *Free Association, 6*(37): 28–55 [reprinted in 2000 in *Tongued with Fire: Groups in Experience*. London: Karnac].

Moore, Y. (2009). Thoughts on representation in therapy of Holocaust survivors. *International Journal of Psychoanalysis, 90*(6): 1373–1391.

Noack, A. (2011). Introduction to Part VI, "The numinous and the unknown". In: E. Hopper & H. Weinberg (Eds.), *The Social Unconscious in Persons, Groups, and Societies: Volume 1: Mainly Theory*, (pp. 289–319). London: Karnac.

CHAPTER THREE

Aspects of the social unconscious reflected in traditional folktales: the case of the Druze community in Israel

Ravit Raufman

T his chapter examines some of the ways in which a traditional folk-tale of a particular ethnic community functions in the social unconscious of the members of it. Focusing on the unique situation of the Druze in Israel, I will discuss the Druze version(s) of the world-wide tale "The Wolf and the Kids", and some of the ways in which the Druze version(s) show various unconscious conflicts, desires, and dynamics, which can be understood in terms of their foundation matrix.

Psychoanalysis and folklore

The idea to use folklore products for the exploration of the human mind and its vicissitudes is as old as psychoanalysis itself. Following Freud's claim that "folklore has adopted a quite different method of research, and yet it has reached the same results as psychoanalysis" (Freud, 1913d), several psychoanalysts have examined the ways in which myths and fairy tales reveal important knowledge of the psychic life of human beings. For example, Karl Abraham (1913) viewed myths as retained fragments from what he and other scholars of the day called the "infantile psychic life of the race", and claimed that "the dream is the myth of the individual" (p. 72). Using folklore products in order to compare the psychic life of the individual and that of the "race", Cheney (1927) noted that the mental development of the individual repeats the stages of the mental development of the race, arguing that, essentially, myths were the manifestations of a primitive mind (p. 199). Of course, the notion of "race" is no longer used and should no longer be used in this way, at least not without qualification and specification. Ernest Jones (1930) stated that ". . . the study of survivals in folklore can be usefully supplemented by the study of survivals in living individuals" (p. 224).

Special attention should be given to the fairy tale genre of folklore products. Fairy tales are considered to be saturated by "primary" unconscious processes. For example, Bruno Bettelheim (1976) applied mainly Freudian concepts to the elucidation of fairy tales. Marie-Louis von Franz (1978) and Erich Neumann (1976) used Jungian perspectives in order to explain the hidden, unconscious meanings of these tales. One of the difficulties in applying classical psychoanalytic theory to the understanding of all folklore products, is the assumption that the theory is universally applicable (Dundes, 1987, p. 23). Actually, this is also true of some anthropological theory. For example, Dundes quotes Adolf Bastian's suggestion that the psychic unity of mankind produced identical elementary ideas, and Levy-Bruhl's belief that the logical structure of the mind is the same in all human societies. However, these approaches do not acknowledge the existence of a social unconscious. Even Freud, who developed his theory from his experience of individual treatment, and referred to the unconscious as in part an individualistic brain-based concept, claimed that a "national character" can be identified. Although Dundes (1975) did not deny the idea of a national character, he argued that a national character is a post-natal trait, acquired through the mediation of culture.

The group analytic approach considers folklore products as stretching beyond the individual, and as belonging to the "folk", or to a certain social group or society, and not as attributable to a single person. This allows the examination of folklore products in terms of the Foulksian "social unconscious" or more precisely the "foundation matrix" of a particular society, as well as the classical Jungian "collective unconscious" of all mankind (Raufman & Weinberg, 2014).[1]

Foulkes referred to the foundation matrix as "the pre-existing community . . . between the members [of it], founded [ultimately] on the basis that they are all human" (Foulkes, 1975, p. 212). Some elements of the foundation matrix of a particular society are based on the social, cultural, and communicational arrangements that are typical of that specific society, and some elements are based on the species Homosapiens, and, therefore, are likely to be universal (Hopper & Weinberg, 2011, p. xlvii).

The tale of "The Wolf and the Kids"

In order to discuss the unique characteristics of the Druze versions, it is important to view it in comparison to the "international tale-type" (or the Grimms' version, which is the most popular one) of "The Wolf and the Kids", as follows.

A mother goat leaves her kids at home while she ventures into the forest to find food. Before she leaves, she warns them about the evil wolf who will try to sneak into the house and gobble them up. The evil wolf will pretend to be their mother and convince the kids to open the door. The kids will be able to recognise their true mother by her white feet and sweet voice. In some versions, the kids fail to recognise the wolf and open the door. In others they refuse to open the door, but the wolf breaks down the door and gobbles up all the kids, except the youngest, who hides and tells his mother what happened when she returns. She cuts open the wolf's belly, and the kids spring out miraculously unharmed. In some versions, they fill the wolf's belly with rocks, and when the wolf wakes up thirsty, he goes to the river to drink, but falls in and drowns under the weight of the rocks.

This tale, which is found in many cultural regions, has been broadly discussed and investigated (El-Shamy, 1999; Espinosa, 1946–1947; Goldberg, 2009; Marzolph, 1984, 2005; Rölleke, 1983; Uther, 2004, 2008). From a psychoanalytic perspective, several interpreations of it have been suggested. For example, Plassmann (1983) suggested that the tale be understood as containing the precise representation of the origin and resolution of neurotic anxiety. The defensive process, which is clinically well known from conditions of anxiety neurosis and phobia, serves to re-establish the mother–child relationship. Róheim (1953) emphasised the cannibalistic impulses in the tale, as well as castration anxiety. Peterson (2011) viewed the tale as an illustration of the importance of metabolising old introjects. Schnell (2003) thought that the main theme of the tale was the development of potential intrapsychic and interpsychic space.

"The Goat and the Ghoulah" is a Druze version of "The Wolf and the Kids". A Ghoulah is a popular supernatural character in Arabic folklore (Bushnag, 1986; Muhawi & Kanaana, 1989; Reynolds, 2007). The most comprehensive of the many versions of "The Goat and the Ghoulah" that are common among the Israeli Druze is as follows.

The goat and the Ghoulah lived together in peace and friendship. They loved and helped one another up until the day when the goat gave birth to five kids. The Ghoulah, who had no children of her own, began to be jealous of the goat. The goat was afraid that the Ghoulah would hurt her kids, so she built a door made of iron at the entrance to the house. Each day, the goat went out to fetch food for her kids, and ordered the kids not to open the door to anyone.

One day, the Ghoulah followed the goat, and when she had gone the Ghoulah entered the goat's backyard, knocked on the door, disguised her voice, and said to the kids: "I'm your mother, the goat; open the door."

The kids peeked out and replied: "You are not our Mother. Our Mother is green."

The Ghoulah went away and painted herself green. The day after, the goat went off to find food, as usual. The Ghoulah returned, disguised her voice and said to the kids:

"I am your Mother. I am green. Please open the door."

The kids peeked out and replied: "You are not our Mother. Our Mother is yellow."

The Ghoulah went away and painted herself yellow. The next day she came to the goat's house, disguised her voice and said to the kids: "I am your Mother. I am yellow. Please open the door."

The kids peeked out and replied: "You are not our Mother. Our Mother is red."

The Ghoulah then became angry. She took an iron rod and broke down the door. The kids were so scared, they scampered all around the house, but she caught them and swallowed four of them. The fifth kid managed to escape and hid in a pot.

In the evening, the goat came back, saw that the door was broken and found her little son hiding, terrified and frightened, in the pot. She asked him: "Where are your brothers?" He told her all about the Ghoulah.

The goat was furious and went straight to the Ghoulah. She challenged her to compete in a heads battle, but the Ghoulah refused, since she didn't have horns and the goat did. The goat then offered to make the Ghoulah a pair of horns. She went home, made a pair of horns out of dough and put them on the Ghoulah's head. Then they climbed to the top of a big rock and started the head-to-head combat, but very soon the Ghoulah's horns broke, since they were made out of dough. This is how the goat overpowered the Ghoulah with her horns. She then cut open the Ghoulah's belly, took her kids out, and they all lived happily ever after.

Several characteristics of the Druze versions of "The Goat and the Ghoulah" compared to the international tale-type of "The Wolf and the Kids"

A comparison between the international tale-type of "The Wolf and the Kids" and the Druze versions of "The Goat and the Ghoulah" suggests that:

1. In each version there is a requirement to identify the right parent.
2. In each version it is necessary to differentiate between friend and foe.
3. In most versions of this tale, the evil character is represented by a wolf (see, for example, Stephan, 1923); in the Druze versions, the wolf is replaced by a Ghoulah.
4. Whereas there is a complete dichotomy between the victim and the carnivore in most versions of this tale, in the Druze versions the goat and the Ghoulah have a friendly relationship, at least until the moment when the goat gives birth to her kids, while this is not the case in "The Wolf and the Kids".
5. Whereas the wolf does not have any specific reason to be vicious in most other versions of this tale, in the Druze versions, each creature has an equal opportunity to be good.
6. The Druze versions are more sympathetic in their portrayal of the Ghoulah, providing an explanation for her dangerous behaviour: she is jealous because she could not bear children of her own. `

7.   The good neighbourly relations between the goat and the Ghoulah do not last forever: when the goat gives birth to her kids, the Ghoulah becomes furious and dangerous.

Some interpretations of the Israeli Druze versions of the tale, and their implications for understanding the social unconscious of the Druze people

From a group analytic perspective, it is possible to understand several aspects of the Israeli Druze version(s) of the tale in terms of the foundation matrix and the social unconscious of the Druze people. Focusing on the unique characteristics of versions of a tale as told by a certain ethnic community is consistent with the idea that folklore is modified to fit local ideologies and world views, and, therefore, it is important to study it in the context of a specific community (Dundes, 1989, p. 73; Raufman, 2011).

In the first instance it is essential to provide some information about the life of the Druze in Israel. The Israeli Druze are one of the many minorities in Israel. They live in a unique and complex situation. The Druze are a monotheistic religious community, which emerged during the eleventh century from Ismailism. Druze beliefs incorporate several elements from Abrahamic religions, Gnosticism, Neoplatonism, and other philosophies. More than 100,000 Druze live in Israel, mainly in the north of the country. In Lebanon, Syria, and Israel, the Druze have official recognition as a separate religious community with its own religious court system. Although they have a strong community feeling in which they identify themselves as related to one another even across the borders of countries, the Druze are known for their loyalty to the countries they reside in. This puts the Israeli Druze in a complex situation, especially in times of conflicts and wars in the Middle East. On the one hand, the Druze share common linguistic and cultural characteristics with the Arab world, but, on the other, they have remained loyal to Israeli Jewish society since the establishment of the State of Israel in 1948. In fact, the Druze are Arabic-speaking citizens of Israel who serve in the Israel Defence Forces. Despite their practice of blending with dominant groups in order to avoid persecution, the Druze have had a history of brave resistance to occupying powers, and they have at times enjoyed more freedom than most other groups living in the Levant. The Druze faith is said to abide by Islamic principles, but they tend to be separatist in their treatment of Druze-hood, and their religion differs from mainstream Islam on a number of fundamental points. The Druze broke off from Islam during the eleventh century and since then they have been subjected to persecution by Muslims (Atashe, 1995; Ben-Dor, 1979; Firro, 2001; Parsons, 2000). The Druze have remained loyal to Israeli Jewish society, as part of their loyalty to the countries they reside in. However, they share many characteristics with the Arab world. Clearly, the Druze have developed a complex, if not contradictory, social identity, based on their unique socio-cultural-political status within the Middle East. Their social identity is composed of a variety of national, social, cultural, political, and linguistic elements.

The relationship between the goat and the Ghoulah and features of the Druze social unconscious

The fact that the Druze version(s) of the tale present a friendly relationship between the goat and the Ghoulah until the moment the goat gives birth to her kids can be understood in terms of the Druze religious principle of loving, respecting, and honouring others (Raufman, 2011). The Druze religion is focused on justice and probity, requiring people to distinguish between good and evil and between truth and falsehood (Atashe, 1995, p. 12; Firro, 1982; Talal & Abi-Sakra, 2001). The Druze versions of the tale begin by giving each creature an equal opportunity to be good. The Druze versions also provide an explanation for the Ghoulah's cruel behaviour: she is jealous because she could not bear children of her own, which shows an awareness of her inner feelings of jealousy and misery.

The deviation from the absolute dichotomy between good and evil suggests a more flexible, tolerant attitude towards moral values, qualities that the Druze attribute to themselves. Generosity and tolerance, emphasising the importance of being good neighbours to other communities in Israel, are important values among the Druze (Atashe, 1995, p. 164). The good relations between the goat and the Ghoulah is a good example of how folklore narratives reflect values that are important to the society in which they are told and which preserves them. This might be understood in terms of the *cultural unconscious*

(Pines, 2009; Spector-Person, 1992), which emphasises the importance of the internalisation of values, norms, and other essential elements of the culture of a particular society, which is one of the key dimensions of the foundation matrix (Hopper & Weinberg, 2011, p. xxvi).

The transition from friendship to hostility (as seen in the facts that the good neighbourly relations between the goat and the Ghoulah did not last forever, and when the goat gave birth to her kids, the Ghoulah became furious and dangerous) can be understood in terms of social dimension of the Druze foundation matrix. The situation of the Druze community in Israel is multi-faceted, in spite of their efforts to co-exist peacefully with other groups. For example, the religious schism in the eleventh century and the subsequent history of persecution was a severe social trauma. Scholz (2011, p. 276) has discussed the role of traumatic events in shaping a group's social structure, referring to how it can bring together the powerful and the powerless, raising high emotions, and breaking down the legitimacy of status differentials. Especially important are "chosen traumas" in which, seemingly independent of time and space, a historical fact comes to define both the inside and the outside of a group (Volkan, 1999). People to whom this event is meaningful and who participate in remembering it in a specific way, that is, how it is perceived and felt, become members of the given group, while those who do not become marginalised from the core of it, perhaps becoming "outsiders", and certainly in danger of being scapegoated (Volkan, 1999, p. 276).

Mental organization, trauma, and the social world

The chaos that occurs after the wolf enters the dwelling can be understood as a consequence of the mother's departure from it (Raufman & Yigael, in press). The mother's departure and the subsequent appearance of the wolf are a "cumulative trauma" (Hopper, 2003). Although the mother needs to detach from the baby, so that the baby can begin a process of differentiation and individuation from the mother, and establish a sense of separateness as a subject, in this tale these processes are exaggerated and harsh.

The tale echoes one of the most primary situations in human development, related to the basic differentiation between inside and outside, helpful and harmful, "me" and "not me", and between what is allowed to enter the mental system and that which is forbidden. It describes the difficulty of identifying the dangers that exist outside the self, those elements that threaten to penetrate it (i.e., the wolf/ Ghoulah), as well as the problems of creating primary and secondary defence mechanisms (i.e., the attempts to defend against the wolf/Ghoulah, which may be perceived as dangers emerging from the outside as well as the inside). Raufman and Yigael (in press) describe *hiding* and *escaping* as primary and secondary defences against the anxieties caused by the penetration of the "wolf" into the mental realm. However, these defences are developed in a social context, as a result of events that take place outside the self.

The Druze social trauma and the collective memory of it

The importance of community and collectivity is especially salient in traditional Arab societies such as that of the Druze. An examination of Arabic folktales in comparison to European ones reveals the central place of the collectivity in Arab traditional societies. The development of the defence mechanisms of the individual in such societies is likely to be related to specific social traumas. The main trauma dealt with in the Druze tales about the goat and Goulah are not perceived only in terms of the mother's departure from the realm that she shared with her offspring, but also in terms of the collective memory of social trauma. For example, the Druze schism from Islam, which is associated with separation and loss. It is possible to view the relations between the Ghoulah and the goat in the Druze version of "The Wolf and the Kids" in terms of this break, since the Druze and the Muslims—in a manner similar to the Ghoulah and the goat—used to be "friends" before the Ghoulah became hostile (Parsons, 2000, p. 13). This is part of the Druze's collective memory. Collective memories can be defined as the representations of the past that the members of a system collectively adopt (Kansteiner, 2002). These representations contribute to the formation of a coherent narrative of the history of the social system. In fact, Weinberg (2007) argued that collective memories of social trauma should be regarded as the building blocks of the social unconscious of the members of a particular social system, primarily because they shape the identity of the system, and, therefore, the social identities of its members (Halbwachs, 1992; Hopper &

Weinberg, 2011, p. xxxviiii). I would suggest that folktales are a kind of a narrative implicitly aimed at conceptualising and constructing various aspects of collective memory.

The relations between the Druze and other communities in Israel

The characteristics of the Druze versions of the wolf and the kids, and especially the way in which issues of belonging and identification are emphasised in these versions, can also be viewed in light of the entangled relationship between the Druze and other ethnic communities in Israel. The Druze people consider their faith to be a new interpretation of the three monotheistic religions: Judaism, Christianity, and Islam. Their mentors and prophets come from all three religions, and include Jethro and Moses (Judaism), John the Baptist and Jesus of Nazareth (Christianity), and Salman the Persian and Mohammed (Islam). Therefore, it is not surprising that the identification test, in which the kids are required to identify their mother and distinguish her from any other creature, plays a central role in these narratives. The ideas that narratives are not solely for the purpose of telling a good story, but also involve a communicative intent (Labov, 1972; Rigney, 1992), help to explain why a story that reflects issues of identification and identity preoccupies the Druze community in Israel.

In discussing the foundation matrix, Foulkes describes persons as well as societies as units that are consistently under construction by communication. Expanding on this idea, Scholz posed the questions: how do groups, or systems of groups, form and maintain themselves? How do the members develop a sense of we-ness, recognising each other as belonging together and excluding others? Scholz views this as an ongoing process, but, at any given moment, it always has a specific shape, which undoubtedly can be described as an historical phenomenon (Hopper & Weinberg, 2011, p. 270). No doubt, fairy tales can be viewed as a way to narrate and communicate a sense of we-ness and belonging. The Druze versions exemplify the way in which the unconscious of a certain society takes its own shape in a way which is different, but, at the same time, similar to other cultural traditions.

The sense of identity of other minorities in Israel is much stronger than that of the Druze, as these other groups are part of the wider

Arab world, and part of the Palestinian political community. The Druze community in Israel suffers from a sense of psychological "uncertainty". It is not surprising that this group would preserve tales in which one of the main issues is the question: "Who is our mother, and who is not?" It is important to explore not only the origins of tales told by certain societies, but also the use of those tales at various times and places. The Druze versions of "The Wolf and the Kids" are told very frequently, and are transferred from one generation to another. Old people tell it, as do young ones.

Winnicottian ideas regarding the use of an object and the transitional phenomena are relevant in that the Druze use this tale as a transitional object, which helps mediate between fantasies and external reality. If it is to be used in this way, the object must necessarily be real in the sense of being part of shared reality, not a bundle of projections (Winnicott, 1969). The Druze use a well-known folktale, that has existed for centuries, and re-create it for their own purposes. The tale, in its turn, functions in various ways, conscious as well as unconscious. The tale reflects the psychological uncertainty of the Druze and, at the same time, helps strengthen their social identity.

Identifying the right parent—to whom should we open the door?

Le Roy (1994) argues that foundation matrices differ in terms of how they spell out such basic dimensions as family systems, gender relations, the relationship between generations, and, moreover, the understanding of inside and outside the cultural group: who belong to "us" and who is "not us" (Scholz, 2011, p. 270). The Druze in Israel have many traits in common with their Arab neighbours, and have no distinct physical characteristics that would distinguish them from the members of another ethnic community. The identification test in the tale deals with questions such as "What does our mother *look* like?", and "To *whom* should we open the door?" The test presents a pivotal challenge of differentiating one ethnic group in society from another. The Druze versions use the colours red, green, and yellow in order to recognise the mother goat. When the kids tell the Ghoulah that their mother is green, yellow, and red (colours which appear in the Druze flag), they are, in fact, declaring their belonging and loyalty to Druze society and religion. Actually, the Druze flag has five colours—green, yellow, red, white, and blue—and yet only three of these colours appear in the identification test. A possible answer to the question why the white and blue are not included in the tale is that white and blue are the colours of the Israeli flag, which officially has been adopted by the Druze people. The crucial importance of the identification test, which allows only family members to enter the house and forbids the penetration of strangers, can also be understood in light of the fact that the Druze religion is closed to converts. No member of any other religion can become Druze.

Another central detail in the tale of the wolf and the kids, in all of its versions, is that after being swallowed by the wolf, the kids are rescued. Whereas this happy ending appears in all of the versions around the world (as well as in many other fairy tales), in the context of the Druze society it attains a special meaning, because the Druze believe in the transmigration of the soul and reincarnation. This plot detail illustrates the possibility of coming back to life after being annihilated. This might make this folktale readily acceptable in the Druze society.

The identification test is especially important in the context of the values in Druze culture concerning the protection of the house and the land. In order to prevent the Ghoulah from entering her house, the goat in the tales builds an extremely strong door, made of iron. Whereas this plot detail is cross-cultural and found in different versions of the tale, it is usually understood in terms of the need to protect the kids, or to teach them how to protect themselves by learning how to differentiate good from bad. However, abandoning the house and the land is perceived by the Druze as a betrayal of a major value (Atashe, 1995, pp. ix, xi, xiii). The attempt made by the kids to prevent the Ghoulah from entering their house might be understood not only as a way of rescuing themselves from being swallowed by the Ghoulah, but also as a metaphor for the concept of defending the house and the land against all comers.

Conclusion

Analysing the Druze versions of the tale "The Wolf and the Kids" in the light of social and cultural dimensions of the foundation matrix, taking into consideration concepts developed through the study of the social unconscious, reminds us of the communicative functions of folktales that are transmitted from one generation to another. This is in line with Rigney's idea, that narratives "should be seen in the first instance as a communicative act carried out by a narrator who wishes to convey information about a certain set of events to someone else" (Rigney, 1992, p. 267). Following this, Rühi states that a narrative is not just a representation of real or imagined events, but carries the function of making people see a set of events as something else from a particular perspective (Rühi, 2000, p. 68). The Druze versions discussed in this chapter can be viewed as a communicative act, conveying information regarding aspects which are crucial for the Druze community in Israel, such as the question of to whom we belong, whom can we trust, as well as relating to one's neighbours and defending one's home and land.

Scholz referred to the way in which language and narration can bridge longer distances. The family members share memories and tell stories. These repeated stories are about how our "we" is constructed. The underlying message is: "That is how it was, before you were here. That is how it is done with us, we are like that and you—as a part of us—are like that". Thus, the child is made a member of the group and obtains words for the already existing connections. Welzer (2002) spells out Halbwachs' notion of collective communicative memory, which is passed on in the families and is based on its "talks"—which means it has its limits in the oral tradition of the family (Hopper & Weinberg, 2011, p. 275). The Druze versions of the folktale about the wolf and the kids is a creative way to transfer values, ideas, fears, and hopes from one generation to another. As Hopper puts it, the socially unconscious mind involves the possibility of creativity and creation. Even the ability and willingness to exercise the transcendent imagination is an action of an interrelational person. In other words: hope is a collective virtue (Hopper, in Hopper & Weinberg, 2011, p. xxxiii).

Note

1. For a discussion of the differences between the social unconscious and the classical concept of the collective unconscious, see Hopper and Weinberg, 2011. Fairy tales can also be considered in terms of the sociological concept of habitus, although this is beyond the scope of the present chapter.

References

Abraham, K. (1913). *Dreams and Myths: A Study in Race Psychology. Nervous and Mental Disease Monograph Series, No. 15.* New York: The Journal of Nervous and Mental Health Publishing.

Atashe, Z. (1995). *Druze and Jews in Israel. A Shared Destiny?* Brighton, UK: Sussex Academic Press.

Bettelheim, B. (1976). *The Uses of Enchantment: The Meaning and Importance of Fairy Tales.* New York: Knopf.

Ben-Dor, G. (1979). *The Druze in Israel. A Political Study, Political Innovation and Integration in a Middle Eastern Minority.* Jerusalem: Magnes Press.

Bushnag, I. (1986). *Arab Folktales.* New York: Pantheon Books.

Cheney, C. O. (1927). The psychology of mythology. *Psychiatric Quarterly,* 1: 190–209.

Dundes, A. (1975). *Analytic Essays in Folklore.* The Hague: Mouton.

Dundes, A. (1987). *Parsing through Customs: Essays by a Freudian Folklorist.* Madison, WI: University of Wisconsin Press.

Dundes, A. (1989). *Folklore Matters.* Knoxville, TN: University of Tennessee Press.

El-Shamy, H. (1999). *Tales Arab Women Tell.* Bloomington, IN: Indiana University Press.

Espinosa, A. M. (1946–1947). *Cuentos populares españoles* (3 vols). Madrid: Instituto Antonio de Nebrija de Filologia.

Firro, K. (1982). The Druze in Israel. *Occasional Papers in the Middle East,* 6: 39–46.

Firro, K. (2001). *The Druze in the Jewish States.* Leiden: E. J. Brill.

Foulkes, S. H. (1975). A short outline of the therapeutic process in group analytic psychotherapy. *Group Analysis,* 8: 59–63.

Freud, S. (1913d). The occurrence in dreams of material from fairy tales. In: *S. E.,* 12: 279–288. London: Hogarth.

Goldberg, C. (2009). The Wolf and the Kids (ATU 123) in international tradition. In: *Erzählkultur, Beiträge zur kulturwissenschaftlichen Erzählforschung. Hans-Jörg Uther zum 65. Geburtstag* (pp. 277–291). Berlin: Walter de Gruyter.

Halbwachs, M. (1992). *On Collective Memory.* London: Penguin.

Hopper, E. (2003). *Traumatic Experience in the Unconscious Life of Groups.* London: Jessica Kingsley.

Hopper, E., & Weinberg, H. (Eds.). (2011). *The Social Unconscious in Persons, Groups, and Societies. Volume I: Mainly Theory.* London: Karnac.

Jones, E. (1930). Psychoanalysis and folklore. In: *Jubilee Congress of the Folk-Lore Society: Papers and Transactions* (pp. 220–237). London: William Glaisher.

Kansteiner, W. (2002). Finding meaning in memory: methodological critique of collective memory studies. *History and Theory, 41*: 179–197.

Labov, W. (1972). *Language in the Inner City. Studies in the Black English Vernacular*. Philadelphia, PA: University of Pennsylvania Press.

Le Roy, J. (1994). Group analysis and culture. In: D. Brown & L. Zinkin (Eds.), *The Psyche and the Social World* (pp. 180–201). London: Routledge.

Marzolph, U. (1984). *Typologie des persischen Volksmarchens. Beiruter Texte und Studien 31*. Beriut: Orient-Institut der Deutschen Morgänlandischen Gesellschaft; (German Edition). Weisbaden: In Komission Bei Franz Steiner Verlag.

Marzolph, U. (2005). Narrative strategies in popular literature. A lecture given in the Folklore Department, University of Haifa, Israel.

Muhawi, I., & Kanaana, S. (1989). *Speak Bird, Speak Again: Palestinian Arab Folktales*. Berkeley, CA: University of California Press.

Neumann, E. (1976). *Amor and Psyche*. Princeton, NJ: Princeton University Press.

Parsons, L. (2000). *The Druze between Palestine and Israel 1947–49*. Basingstoke: Macmillan.

Peterson, C. A. (2011). Pronouns and progress: a psychoanalytic primer. *Psychoanalytic Review, 98*(4): 515–530.

Pines, M. (2009). Personal communication concerning the "cultural unconscious". In: E. Hopper & H. Weinberg (Eds.), *The Social Unconscious in Persons, Groups, and Societies. Volume I: Mainly Theory*. London: Karnac, 2011.

Plassmann, R. (1983). Psyche: *Zeitschrift für Psychoanalyse und ihre Anwendungen, 37*(9): 841–846.

Raufman, R. (2011). Defending the house, relating to the neighbors: the Druze versions of ATU 123 "the wolf and the kids". *Folklore, 122*(3): 250–263.

Raufman, R., & Weinberg, H. (2014). Two forms of blindness in the social unconscious as expressed in literary texts, *Group-Analysis, 47*(2): 159–174.

Raufman, R., & Yigael, Y. (in press). The wonder-tale's point of view of the primary psyche. *American Journal of Psychoanalysis*, in press.

Reynolds, D. F. (2007). *Arab Folklore. A Handbook*. Berkeley, CA: Greenwood Press.

Rigney, A. (1992). The point of stories: on narrative communication and its cognitive functions. *Poetic Today, 13*: 263–83.

Róheim, G. (1953). The Wolf and the Seven Kids. *Psychoanalytic Quarterly*, 22: 253–256.

Rölleke, H. (1983). August Stöbers Einfluß auf die Kinder-und Hausmärchen der Brüder Grimm, Zur Textgenese der KHM 5 und 15. *Fabula*, 24: 11–20.

Rühi, Ş. (2000). The bone motif and lambs in the Turkish folktale 'The Reed Door'. *Asian Folklore Studies*, 59(1): 59–77.

Schnell, M. (2003). Das Geisslein im Uhrenkasten und die Frau im Kleiderschrank. *Analytische Psychologie*, 34(3): 173–191.

Scholz, R. (2011). The foundation matrix and the social unconscious. In: E. Hopper & H. Weinberg (Eds.), *The Social Unconscious in Persons, Groups, and Societies. Volume I: Mainly Theory* (pp. 265–285). London: Karnac.

Spector-Person, E. (1992). Romantic love: at the intersection of the psyche and the cultural unconscious. In: T. Shapiro & R. Emde (Eds.), *Affect Psychoanalytic Perspective*. New York: International Universities Press.

Stephan, S. H. (1923). Palestinian animal stories and fables. *Journal of the Palestinian Oriental Society*, 3: 167–90.

Talal, F., & Abi-Sakra, Z. (Eds.) (2001). *The Druze Heritage. An Annotated Bibliography*. London: Royal Institute for Inter-Faith Studies.

Uther, H. J. (2004). *The Types of International Folktales. A Classification and a Bibliography*, Parts 1–3. FF Communications 284–6. Helsinki: Academia Scientiarum Fennica.

Uther, H. J. (2008). *Handbuch zu den "Kinder und Hausmärchen" der Brüder Grimm*. Berlin: Walter de Gruyter.

Volkan, V. D. (1999). *Das Versagen der Diplomatie* [The Failure of Diplomacy]. Gießen: Psychosozial.

Von Franz, M. L. (1978). *An Introduction to the Psychology of Fairy Tales*. Irving, TX: Spring.

Weinberg, H. (2007). So what is this social unconscious anyway? *Group Analysis*, 40(3): 307–322.

Welzer, H. (2002). *Das kommunikative Gedächtnis* [The Communicative Memory]. München: C. H. Beck.

Winnicott, D. W. (1969). The use of an object. *International Journal of Psychoanalysis*, 50: 711–716.

PART II
FOUNDATION MATRICES

The German social unconscious: second generation perpetrator symptoms in organisations and groups*

Gerhard Wilke

We have detailed knowledge about victims of traumatising historical events, and colleagues such as Dina Wardi have written movingly about the children of survivors (Wardi, 1992). What we know less well are the phenomena associated with perpetrators and their children. It has been politically incorrect to ask the question whether a perpetrator society, like Germany, can be regarded as traumatised. In this contribution, I want to pose the following questions: first, in what meaningful way can it be shown that post-war Germany is a traumatised society? Second, what evidence is there that some, if not all, organisations are location points for repressed and encapsulated unconscious dynamics associated with the "forbidden knowledge" of the trauma of a whole society descending into barbarism? Third, why is it necessary to re-examine the social unconscious of German society with the help of trauma theory?

---

* Some of the ideas presented in this chapter are developed in Wilke (2014), *The Art of Group Analysis in Organisations*. London: Karnac.

The socially unconscious mind of a perpetrator
society as a traumatised mind

German society and its organisations are led now by a generation that is not guilty by deed but feels ashamed and guilty by association with their parents. The impact of the Second World War, the Nazi and Communist dictatorships, and the Cold War is an "introject" in the minds of many living Germans. The transgenerational transmission of a bad rather than a good we-object has a long history in Germany. Norbert Elias, in his 1992 book, listed the developmental breaks that made Germany different from other nations since the Protestant Reformation. He argued that the abortive unification of the country in 1871 and the subsequent catastrophic and self-destructive two world wars prevented Germans from securing a civilised identity rooted in an uncomplicated and proud identification with the nation as a good we-object. The story of Germany is, therefore, one of succeeding generations being carriers of a form of social trauma for the preceding one. The feeling that Germans want to be dissociated from their belonging group and their parents is not new, but dramatically different in the quality of the experience for those who carry this inheritance since 1945, due to the uniquely barbaric nature of the holocaust.

The symptoms of "socially unconscious" guilt and shame and the associated generational boundary confusion in post-war Germany have tended to be analysed moralistically, not empathically, lest the responsibility for the holocaust be watered down by the admission that many Germans suffered, too. The inability of the perpetrator generation to mourn their victims and show remorse has been the focus in the psychoanalytic literature. The maturation problems of the post-war generation in West Germany was analysed by the Mitscherlichs as an extension of a collective sense of guilt and inability to mourn (Mitscherlich & Mitscherlich, 1967). Partly as a result of this work, it has so far been forbidden to think that a large number of the perpetrators were simultaneously "Hitler's willing helpers" and traumatised by the terrible events at the Eastern Front, the nights under Allied bombs, the forceful removal of whole populations from the East, and the loss of several millions of unmourned family members. It is time to recognise these traumas for what they are, lest the repressed shall return to haunt us—which it occasionally shows signs of doing since the fall of the Berlin Wall with the rise of Neo-Nazis in the old East Germany.

The thesis put forward here is that members of the "Nazi genera-tion", who were traumatised by war and dislocation, encapsulated any memory associated with the repression of all opposition, euthanasia and the persecution of the Jews and other minorities, and their own collusion, together with their own experiences of the war, in the recesses of their disturbed minds, making it inaccessible to words and conscious reflection. The encapsulated feelings associated with the trauma of war became, instead, available for transgenerational trans-mission into the next generation. In the service of going on living, perpetrators, if they were not fully blown psychopaths in the Gestapo and the parts of the SS associated with the genocide, dealt with the traumatising nature of the events they took part in, just like any other traumatised person—they unconsciously "selected" some of their children to carry the feelings they could no longer handle on their behalf and thereby deprived them of the right to their own true self and a good parental and societal object. Social trauma is social trauma, in a psychological sense, with respect both to victims and perpetrators.

My generation asked in vain: "Daddy, what did you do in the war?" In fact, the need to repeatedly ask this question could be inter-preted as a symptom of social trauma that has been passed on, through projection, to the next generation for mental processing and working through. It is this passing on of responsibility to a generation that had not committed the evil deeds, and the psychological defences against this burden, that surface in post-war German organisations and therapeutic groups. Martin Schmidbauer, a prominent individual and group therapist, tried to open up the whole topic of trauma in German society in his 1998 book, the title of which translates as "What was the Matter with Dad? The Trauma of the War" (Schmidbauer, 1998). He lists the reasons why we can talk of the traumatisation of German frontline soldiers and home front civilians, despite their direct or indirect involvement in the holocaust and in causing the Second World War. The arguments he puts forward are: first, that people exposed to repeated situations of "helplessness" in the face of death are bound to develop symptoms of traumatisation and pass them on to their children. Second, that the repeated involvement in fighting had a cumulative effect on the psyche of the soldiers, if only to exhaust them and deprive them, over time, of the capacity to feel empathy and understand the suffering of others—again generating a need for transgenerational transmission. Third, that therapy since the

Second World War has shown that the children were projectively put in the role of unconsciously helping to work through the psychic inheritance of the trauma of fighting and being subjected to a brutal war; being a party to genocide in the case of fathers at various fronts, and of having been exposed to bombing, hunger, evacuation, and resettlement in the case of mothers, siblings, and relatives.

In a recent book, *Nazism and War*, the historian Richard Bessel (2004) concluded "it is difficult to imagine a society more profoundly disrupted than that left behind by Nazism". The inheritance was not just physical, but also psychological. Bessel has not considered the unmourned dead at the front, in bombing raids, and during the repatriation of Germans from the eastern provinces by the Red Army and the occupied states under its control. Bruno Bettelheim (1987) wrote about the absence of basic trust in relation to both parental objects in post-war German children and concluded that there was an inappropriate level of unconscious fear of the aggressive parts of the id and, as a reaction formation, a much too severe superego, defending against the wish to express the rage against the fate of having been dealt such bad cards by history. The result is that a sense of self and sense of secure identity are very tenuous. In short, post-war German patients need help with understanding their own story as linked to, but also distinct from, their parent's deeds. They need encouragement to identify with their social unconscious and foundation matrix as their very own—good and bad.

Second generation perpetrators' symptoms

In the light of the extent of historical dislocation experienced by millions of Germans during and after the Second World War, it is justified to re-examine the fate of being a descendant of the perpetrator generation. In the 2007 Foulkes Memorial Lecture in London, I proposed that, as practitioners, we should recognise the existence of "second generation perpetrator symptoms" which we can observe, diagnose, and treat in a clinical context. (Wilke, 2007). I identified the following symptoms.

1. *The absence of a positive identification with the father and presence of a persecuting internal authority figure.* This becomes very apparent

on the group analytic training course in Germany when people use the experiential learning group to "repair" the transference relationship to their individual training analyst. They use the group to slowly separate from the assumption that the aim of the analyst is to avoid making a mistake, lest a mistake results in hurting the dependent patient and shaming the "perpetrator" into being just like a Nazi. Important interactions and joint explorations between the infantilised trainee and the overpowering training analyst seem to have re-created the lack of basic trust between parent and child in post-war homes. It is remarkable how difficult it is for analysts with perpetrator parents to overcome their often terrifying fear of an open and potential space in which patient, group, and analyst learn to make sense together. When trainees on the Group Analytic Course in Germany let go, they frequently discover that they had fathered their father and mothered their mother, and that this failure of dependency, not the actual terrible deeds of their parents, was the source of their own trauma

2. *The displaced resentment against the colluding mother projected on to the We of the national belonging group.* In the transference to the group, post-war children repeatedly dramatise their need of the group as a dependable environmental mother. Consequently, the group, as an object, is viewed as a perfect mother or a persecuting witch. The fear in relating to the group and the analyst is the working through of the oedipal position where group and conductor can be triangulated with each member in the role of an accepted and independent child. The pull towards a dyadic relationship between member and unsafe group mirrors the encapsulated trauma of the merger with the "barbaric" Nazi crowd and a leader who was imagined as benign but turned out to be "malignant", murderous and responsible for the destruction of Germany. This, together with the transgenerational transmission scenario at home, reinforces the dis-eased relationship between the I and the We but also between id–ego and superego in the social unconscious of post-war Germans.

3. *The avoidance of the perpetrator position and the over-identification with perceived victims.* This is very understandable in the post-war situation and parallels the identification of the victims with their aggressors, as a defence against the depression and the rage that

flows from embracing the delegated task of working through the encapsulated (Hopper, 1991) Third Reich on behalf of their parents. The parents were, with very few exceptions, merciless to victims; their descendants have tremendous mercy for the victims and, by implication, are merciless towards their own parents. Both positions share a state of mindlessness and expose what is feared—one's identification with the perpetrator parents. The desire to remain innocent also hides unexpressed envy and aggression towards the idealised victims and their descendants. On analytic training courses, this surfaces in the tendency to repeatedly put authority figures such as training analysts, who embody descent from the victims, into a position where they are asked to absolve the shame and guilt carried by the second-generation perpetrator child. The denial of their own drama sucks them into a dynamic of seeking parent substitutes, the hope being that by identifying with the personification of a better Germany (émigrés and survivors), they can fix their inadequate parents and obtain permission to live their own lives.

4.   *The enactment of a secret wish to be as heroic and grandiose as the perpetrator parents.* This symptom is linked to the thesis of Vamik Volkan's and others that the second and third generation cannot escape carrying introjected behaviour patterns of the Nazi regime in to their own lives (Volkan, 2002). This identification with the perpetrator parents can be malignant or benign. The student movement of 1968 started off as a protest against the authority figures of the 1950s and early 1960s who, with the exception of the returned émigrés, had all colluded with the Nazi regime. It embodied initially a benign search for good leaders and adaptive and helpful groups. The protest movement aimed to transform educational structures and practices rooted in Nazism. However, it soon turned into the feared re-enactment of the political sectarianism of the Weimar Republic, which produced the crisis in the context of which the malignant dictator and the mindless and persecutory mass emerged and offered messianic solutions at the expense of external and internal enemies. In the final state, a minority sect within the student movement became terrorists and took up arms against the democratic state. Both sides, the terrorists and the state authorities, displayed symptoms of Nazi and Communist extremism, ruthlessness, and fanaticism. In the end,

the episode became a stepping-stone in the working through of the socially unconscious inheritance of the Third Reich and consolidated more mature structures in the collective mind of West German civil society. The rage expressed by the terrorists defended against the unconscious delegation of working through the encapsulated traumatogenic material and aimed to cleanse the polluted we-object of the nation through violence and summary executions.

5. Last, but not least, one can sense that *second generation perpetrator children in groups have a need to work on the level of the personal as well as the social unconscious.* Therefore, it is important that group conductors create secure enough boundaries and potential spaces in which the encapsulated traumatogenic material can be enacted and translated from scenic dramatisation into words. The need to work beyond the here and now and the transference of the family group becomes apparent through compulsive attempts to show the whole group and the therapist that the patient or members of the family were able to escape the impact of the Nazi foundation matrix. At such moments, when patients repeatedly try to pro-test their innocence, it is worth opening the story up again and separating out the suffering of the second generation child and the experience of persecution, collusion, and suffering in the perpetrator generation. The task is to avoid collapsing both stories into one and not condemning the descendants for the sins of the fathers.

Working with transgenerational transmission, as Hopper (2003a) has shown convincingly in his work on the social unconscious, allows us to observe and recover this "undigested" psychic material. The group members who lend a voice to the encapsulated social trauma of collective guilt and shame, for which they show a valence, act as if they are really guilty and ashamed in the present (Hopper, 1997, 2003b). They carry split off and unbearable psychic and social mater-ial for the previous generation, and make it possible for past, present, and future to be interlinked in the face of threatening demands and events that evoke loss and, with it, the unmourned and unremem-bered dead. Actually and metaphorically, this is how history is brought to life during a therapeutic process by one or several of the group members who respond to an unconscious need to embody the role of perpetrator, victim, or bystander. This happens when that which has been made socially unconscious in the interaction between perpetrators and their children needs to be taken into account in the re-unfolding of what David Bohm has called the implicate order, which group analysts conceptualise as a re-enactment of a scene associated with the original trauma (Bohm, 2002).

In the German case, at a social systems level, the socially unconscious structure of encapsulated trauma, within an externally successful and internally dislocated and divided society, breaks open in critical moments. This can be seen in the unification of the country or the outbreak of the student revolt in 1968. At a personal level, the implicate order in the minds of second-generation perpetrator children is the sense of being ashamed of their parents. Of course, what perpetrator parents projected into their children varies, but I would argue that the inability to own the encapsulated and frightening parts of their "memory" resulted in the intrusive presence of parts of the parents' psyche in the core identity and self-representation of their children. In a sense, these children had no choice but to develop a "false self" in response to an undependable national "we" and "diseased" parental object. The result of this inversion of the container–contained relationship between parents and children left the post-war generation exposed to the risk of three not very palatable psychological choices: one, to remain identified with the parents and repress the memory of the nation's regression into barbarity through denial or the displacement of the conflict; two, to accept that the descendants of the victors and victims of the Second World War will ask them to complete the work of reparation and remorse on behalf of their parents, and learn to see this as a chance to give birth to an authentic I and We for themselves in relation to the other; three, to remain locked in a generational battle in which the descendants of the perpetrators display a valence for embodying the arrogance, rigidity, and fanaticism of their parents.

Since the 1960s, a series of articles have appeared in analytic journals in Germany exploring whether a specific second generation perpetrator syndrome exists and can be given credence. The answer has, in every case, been no. All the writers have concluded that "Survivor Syndrome" and "Second Generation Syndrome" (Niederland, 1980) are only the result of the unimaginable horror of the holocaust and are appropriate for use in clinical diagnosis. Any comparable set of psychological symptoms in perpetrators and their descendants is, on the other hand, undeserving of the status of a trauma. As if the significance of the one depends on the insignificance of the other. This conclusion is appropriate and correct from a moral and political point of view, but it precludes the proper analytic exploration of the transgenerational phenomena enacted compulsively by the descendants of the perpetrators, indicating that they did have traumatised parents. The "evidence" for the existence of the perpetrators' trauma is borne out in a survey published by the German journal *Psyche* in 2001, evaluating the effectiveness of psychoanalytic treatment. Sixty-three per cent of the sample who sought help from psychoanalysts showed signs of improvement when traumatising events in their early childhood, such as bombing, forced repatriation from their homes, violence at the hands of advancing Russian soldiers, and transgenerational transference material deposited by parents involved in Hitler's racial and military war, was expressed and analysed. In other words, any kind of help or cure depended on allowing the social unconscious to lie on the couch, alongside the inner object representations of the family of origin (Leuzinger-Bohleber, 2001). The study also shows clearly that a consistent set of developmental deficits can be identified in the children of perpetrators, leaving them with a valence to over-identify with the victim position in an attempt to become the loveable, not the hated and rejected, German. Leuzinger-Bohleber's analysis of the survey's results reveals that the transgenerational transference of guilt, shame, and loss make it impossible to verbalise what was traumatising in the relationship between the generations and the analyst and analysand, and that the war and post-war German children invariably resort to enacting this trauma before they can engage in a reflective and reparative process. In other words, the analyst and group therapist has to facilitate a holding environment in which redramatisations of the transgenerational conflict and transference can take place.

Redramatisations of the trauma of the Third Reich

The psychological inheritance of encapsulated trauma in the social unconscious also becomes palpable in many German organisations because post-war children of the perpetrator generation are leaders, followers, and bystanders in them. Let me illustrate how trans-generational transference symptoms, encapsulated in the social unconscious, become visible through consultancy and supervision work in an organisational context in a post-perpetrator society.

Case: The professor of architecture

For the past decade, I have worked with a professor of architecture from the Bauhaus school in Dessau in Germany. He has an office in a West German city and is well known for building synagogues. The specialisation is no accident, as his parents were Auschwitz survivors and he functions within the family as a "memorial candle", and has had to realise his own potential within the confines of this psychological inheritance. I have coached him and consulted with his office on a regular basis and this work has given me a glimpse of a significant parallel process in a post-perpetrator society. In a society that is suffering from the effects of massive social trauma, descendants of victims and perpetrators can become "location points" in the socially unconscious foundation matrix for touching, naming, and enacting social events that become linked and associated with the trauma of persecution and survival.

Psychoanalysts and group analysts know very little about the social unconscious of the foundation matrix of a societal system that is not in acute crisis. Social actors within a society, which resembles a sense of "normality" but is still burdened with undigested and unconscious social trauma, draw on stories, public rituals, and shared collective memories to lend themselves a sense of shared identity and group cohesion. To construct a sense of "normality", certain memories and stories are collusively included and excluded from the "socially acceptable" exchange of words and actions. The taboo subjects in the public dialogue are unconsciously delegated to "selected" social actors, who will express them on behalf of the majority. They have a valence to volunteer for this role because of their own unconscious family history and their minority position within the social system. They unconsciously single themselves out and are chosen by the majority to take on the task of naming what is unnameable. This apparent opposition between insider and outsider helps those who feel themselves to be the normal to maintain a familiar sense of social order. It is the "as if" quality of a re-enactment of something linked to the past, something reminiscent of the perpetrator–victim dynamic in the present, that signifies that socially unconscious processes are at work.

The client whom I mentioned above was captured by such a collusive dynamic. In 2006, the Bauhaus School of Architecture had its centenary celebration and, for this occasion, a Symposium and a Festschrift (commemorative publication) were planned. My client, being the only Jewish member of staff, should perhaps have been asked to write a contribution for the book about the members of the Bauhaus who were driven out by the Nazis, ended up in exile, and became world famous. It is something he is an expert on and such a contribution would have helped him to reclaim his own lost tradition within the Institution. Instead, he was asked to write about the Bauhaus member who collaborated with the Nazis, became famous for establishing the ISO industrial norms, and designed bunkers for the army and the DIN-norms for the bunks in concentration camps. My client was fully conscious of having been delegated the "wrong" task but decided to accept it in order, as he put it, "to use the occasion to put the record straight and remind everyone of what can't be named in everyday life". He wrote his contribution on time and sent it to the editor of the Festschrift. As the anniversary drew nearer he was shown the proofs of the Festschrift and noticed, to his amazement, that his text was not included. When he confronted the editor, he was told that the editorial committee had forgotten to include his manuscript in the book. My client was very upset. On reflection, we decided that the way to deal with this unconscious act of repression was to ask the organising committee of the Symposium to make the "forgotten" contribution the opening lecture. In this way, the repressed was allowed to return in a benign way and the fear of the descendants of the perpetrators of being sucked into unpalatable memory work, on the occasion of the institution's anniversary, was enacted to open up a space for mourning and reparation. The cost to my client was that his version of the past was excluded from the official record of that past. Why? It is still too painful to be remembered in a conscious way, and he retained his role as the "memorial candle" on behalf of the persecuted and killed members of the founder generation of the Bauhaus. In terms of the logic of the social unconscious, it made a terrifying kind of sense that the Jewish member of staff should be delegated to talk about the Nazi past of the institution. Only he could speak without inhibition about the shameful past and thereby protect his German colleagues in the present from the re-enactment of their own trauma—to feel guilty and ashamed on behalf of their own parents.

The same client asked me one day to participate in a project, designed to highlight the fact that the second largest Jewish community in Germany did not have a synagogue forty-five years after the war had ended. Several things had come together. The community itself was reluctant to go public and unpack the suitcases in a place associated with the mass murder of their own relatives. The local political elite had given the community a piece of land in the 1960s and promised large subsidies for the construction of a community centre and place of worship. The snag was that this piece of prime real estate had a secret. Underneath the ground lay the first underground bunker for the Nazi elite, designed to let them carry on their work while the Allies bombed the city. A surveyor's report, after the land had been signed over to the Jewish community, showed that the cost of removing the bunker would be greater than the building of the new synagogue. As a result, nothing happened for almost thirty years, the community built a car park on the land, and created the publicity and exposure it feared by possessing an eyesore in the middle of a historic town centre which repeatedly became the subject of negative publicity.

In the early 1990s, three things changed: my client was driven to add a different object of desire to the collection of new synagogues he had built in the 1980s, a new head of town planning wanted to reopen the case and look with fresh eyes at the project, and the community elected a woman, herself a survivor, as its president, who took the line that the synagogue should be built on top of the bunker, thereby symbolically signifying the community's survival. It was decided to raise public awareness through an unusual architectural project. The final-year students from a top architecture school in Germany and in Israel were invited to visit the site, interview the locals and the community, consult with the planners, and then submit designs for the new synagogue as their diploma project. When the consultative process had ended and the designs were in first draft form, the two student bodies met for a workshop. Integral to this training event was a large group that took place in the cafeteria area of a German university. The seating area for the students was built like a Roman amphitheatre: the shape of the self-contained seating area was a triangle and there were three downward steps to sit on and an empty space in the middle.

The group comprised about sixty-five students and four professors. After a short introduction in which I stated that we had assembled to explore the emotional aspects of the encounter with each other, the site and the task, there was a short silence. As I wondered what the effect on the group would be as we sat in an oedipal triangle, the caretaker of the building stormed into the hall. He somehow sensed that I was the leader, although I was one among many sitting in the triangle, and started shouting at me: "Do you have official permission for this illegal assembly? Wait until the Director gets to hear of this ... Get out ... I will call the director now ... Don't move ... It is disgusting ... I never know what is going on ... in this place."

I did nothing and waited.

There was a very brief standoff between him and the group. Most of the group turned away and stared into the empty space in the centre of the seating area. Suddenly, a German professor stood up and started to shout back: "Of course we have permission, you stupid fool. Stop bothering us. Do your own work and leave us to do ours." The caretaker went away in a huff, the professor sat down with his whole body still shaking. There was again a short silence. The group looked stunned and mesmerised. Another staff member started speaking about the task in hand and wondered whether a synagogue was any different from building a mosque or a church in modern Germany. A German student responded by saying that he was just going to design an empty building which could also be a fire station, what the inhabitants did with it was their business. They had to give meaning to the space he was willing to design, not he. The word fire station was a trigger for another student to say that this project was different, that a synagogue in Germany could never be viewed as a neutral construction. Too many of them had been consumed by fire during "Kristallnacht" in 1938.

The group carried on working like this and it very quickly became clear that there was not so much a differentiation into a German or Israeli sub-group, but splits were opening up around the disagreement of whether the design for this synagogue should resemble a modernist, functional, and rational construction or should take on the shape of an emotional, historically rooted holocaust memorial. These two paradigms established themselves very firmly and were not shifted by the large group for a long time. Towards the end, a third perspective emerged. An in-between sub-group thought that both the modernist and memorial perspective needed to be reflected in the design of this building. The difference between these ways of seeing seemed to be shaped by the influence of childhood experiences. Those who wanted to build a memorial to the holocaust victims had come from homes with parents who had suffered during the Second World War and had talked about it; those who wanted to keep their distance from the history of persecution came from families who had remained silent about the war experiences of the previous generation. The in-between category of students seemed freer to choose their position in the here and now and shared a meaningful history of an emotional contact with the holocaust story during their secondary socialisation at school.

Although it was pleasurable to find this overly neat fit between the design and inner history of Germans and Jews via the family or the school, the really significant event took place at the boundary of the group. While we were working on the emotional dimensions of designing a synagogue inside the group, the caretaker assembled his team and started to move furniture around us in a bizarre and mindless way for the remainder of the session. In a synchronic sequence, they ended their furniture arrangement in such a way that they were back in their original position by the end of the group. Almost simultaneously with the end of the group, the noise surrounding and uniting us, stopped. I was left with just sufficient sound-free time to thank everyone and summarise the major patterns that had emerged during the session. Everyone got up looking like Munch's scream and full of dis-ease about the power of the social unconscious which had driven them to sit in a public forum being surrounded by people who had regressed into a fascist state of mind and redramatised the traumatic scene between the Nazis and their enemies—the Jews and the intellectuals (Bollas, 1991). By moving the furniture, they attacked thinking and wanted to reduce all of us to a state of mindlessness in which the unthinkable could be acted out.

This case material demonstrates many issues mentioned in the introduction of this chapter, including how encapsulated unconscious dynamics associated with the "forbidden knowledge" of the trauma of a whole society can be re-enacted by individuals and groups. It also illustrates the way inner object relations shape reparation in the here and now, and how the attempt to integrate the disconnected parts of the past in the individual and group mind is subject to interlinked pathological and re-creative forces. Joint work in the here and now can tolerate the destructive, self-destructive, and re-creative forces in a shared psychological and social time and space. Elias (1991) showed that the direction of the social group process is potentially always in two directions: widening and deepening the civilising forces; widening and deepening the de-civilising forces. His picture was that of the ground and the related figuration upon it. What is in the foreground and what in the background at any moment in time is not controllable and depends on the dynamic balance of the forces shaping the group process, forces which can ultimately be traced back to the cumulative and evolutionary effect of individual interactions within a socially and psychologically shared context.

Socially unconscious reactions in organisations

The Third Reich in the social unconscious is still kept at bay in many commercial and public sector organisations in Germany by "compulsive" attempts to "contain" the charismatic leader through very strict and rigid bureaucratic controls. The underlying fear of being abused by the leader or of the group losing control is defended against through compulsive boundary control or by seeking a transforming object that is benign. The hope is that by re-enacting the trauma of the relationship between leader and followers, the internalised object relations to the parents and the nation can be repaired.

Extrapolating from my experience as an organisational consultant, I want to make the following observations on how the defence against the fear of the repeated descent into "barbarity" in a post-perpetrator society manifests itself in organisational life in Germany:

1. Change and merger processes are painfully experienced in terms of victims and perpetrators. Separation from established ways of working feel like a redramatisation of the loss of security and dependability which the parents lived through when the idealised "environmental mother" of the massified Nazi state became murderous and self-destructive. In a multi-national company context, Germans tend to volunteer for the role of "refusnik" before others. This seems linked to the post-traumatic societal context. An open and spontaneous expression of what you want signifies a form of collusion with the new order and requires an

unconscious identification with the position of the perpetrator. This is unconsciously forbidden, as it implies an unthinking identification with the bad father.

2. A vision of the future for the organisation is viewed as desirable by Anglo-Saxon business schools and organisations; they see it as a necessary mechanism for staying alive in a competitive environment. Organisational disturbance imposed from the top and visions dreamt up by transformational leaders mean something very different in the social unconscious of Germans and in their organisations. As the German Chancellor Helmut Schmidt put it to consultants who tried to convince him of the need for a vision: "I think people who have visions need to see a doctor." Meaning, I once ended up serving a madman, never again!

3. The losses incurred by restructuring an organisation remind German employees of incomplete mourning process. The loss of holding structures feels traumatising to many people who were born during or immediately after the war. Organisational changes are experienced as annihilation rather than adaptation scenarios by those who carry the unresolved social traumas on behalf of their families. There seems no room for a middle ground, or a compromise. Therefore, relatively small events become catastrophic and threatening. They cannot be taken up as a welcome opportunity for learning and growth. If you like, many Germans are inoculated against "visionary change", lest the self-destruction of German society and its organisations is repeated by succumbing to blind followership or worship of a charismatic leader. This fear makes a difference to the work of managers and management consultant as the objects of leadership and consultation need to find out whether those who have come to offer help can be trusted or will end up being abusive.

4. The dynamic of avoiding the perpetrator position—which is unconsciously identified with the imagined or real Nazi parents—generates a compulsive need to seek the victim or bystander role. The distinction between power and authority is lost as all power is assumed to be abusive. What is absent, until the social unconscious is worked through more thoroughly, is the link between authority and development, dependency and holding. The absence of a good parental object in early childhood and adolescence makes it hard to avoid splitting. It is, therefore,

impossible to see leadership as a social process where power is not located in the leader or the follower, but between them. Even the founding father of group analysis, Foulkes, was not immune to these forces as he conjured up the vision of a conductor of a symphony orchestra, rather than a jazz-band leader, as the role model for the group analyst (Foulkes, 1948). The doubts of Foulkes about the word leader—which means Führer—are part of the post-traumatic condition.

Unification of the nation

The post-war German situation appeared that of a normal society at work, but in the background of all social interactions the encapsulated guilt, shame, and rage against the collective burden of responsibility for the holocaust, the descent into barbarity, and the adoration of the abusive Führer played on many people's minds. Above all, the damage to the parents' self esteem and their capacity to function as containing objects for their children had a retraumatising effect. The outcome of this existential insecurity was the experience of profound helplessness and envy of the victim position. The parents invested their children with the hope of becoming objects that could fix the damaged self. Through this reversal in the generational hierarchy, the oedipal conflict in early childhood and adolescence could not be contained within the boundary of the family and was acted out instead in public at the juncture of significant historical events such as the student revolt or German unification.

The moment of joy, the unification of the country and the fall of the Wall, was, therefore, the beginning of yet another working through process linked to facing up to the consequences of dictatorship, spying, and persecution. The difference was that this time the two parts of Germany cast each other in the role of perpetrators and victims, East Germans seeing their brothers and sisters from the West as colonisers, West Germans perceiving their newly inherited siblings in the East as ungrateful and resentful. Unification blocked the flight of the West Germans into a good European identity and removed the containing split between the good or bad west and east. The process paradoxically opened a space in which it became possible to think that perpetrators, too, are traumatised by setting the world on fire and reaping the destruction of the country. Unification turned into a kind of transition process, helping the Germans to face up to the issue of how the good and the bad Germans can live within one society and lend its members a more secure we identity, which enabled them to resist the re-enactment of another decivilisation process.

The unbloody nature of the unification of the two halves of Germany brought the losses of the Germans to the surface. What united the two Germanys on the socially unconscious level before unification was the "chosen trauma" of the denial of their own suffering and their own losses as a result of the Third Reich. The fall of the Berlin Wall opened a transitional space in which the socially unconscious traces of the holocaust, the Second World War, and the division of the nation could be connected, without the use of the ideological filters of the Cold War. This facilitated a more authentic working through of the shame and guilt associated with the failure to resist the abusive leaders at the helm of the dictatorial systems. Since the fall of the Iron Curtain, it has been possible to rebuild some of the synagogues consumed by the fire of Kristallnacht and to consciously remember what has been done by the Germans in the name of their nation to the Jews, other minorities, occupied countries, and oppositional Germans.

Vamik Volkan's writings on the function of the social unconscious show the apparent pathological nature of transgenerational transmission of traumatic experience as well as the important, and maybe integrating, function they have for the working through of traumatogenic processes which puncture the cohesion and integrity of the belonging group and the individuals in it. In periods of great social stress and psychological dislocation, many individuals and the whole society become absorbed in the compulsive re-enactment of what Volkan calls the "chosen trauma" of the belonging group. They do so to retain a sense of identity and to prevent fragmentation and incorporation. As a reassurance ritual, so to speak, threatened national groups, individuals, and sub-groups within them need to reconnect with their dormant visions of heroic greatness and their fears of overwhelming enemies at the gate. What is unique about German unification is that the enemy is the other half of Germany. The fact that the enemy is within is a re-enactment of the Nazi persecution of the Jews, the Communists, and the mentally handicapped, except, in this re-enactment, it is the German sibling that is cast in the role of the coloniser or the ungrateful "native". The psychological gain is, so far, in the toleration of the tension between the two halves and the patient work of national integration that is beginning to show signs of success. The collectively and selectively "chosen trauma", which lends us an identity and makes up for our sense of individual and collective inadequacy, will speak through us in times of collective dis-stress such as the unification of a country.

In each decade since the end of the war, aspects of the unprocessed chosen trauma were acted out in West Germany. However, since reunification it has become possible to integrate in the psychological inheritance of the Third Reich in a more mature way. It was a significant part of the East German population, a benign Soviet leader, and the German and American leadership that brought about the miracle of an unbloody revolution and facilitated the recovery of a sense of pride in the unified national belonging group.

Conclusion

The unthinkable that I want to make thinkable is that many perpetrators were, for very different reasons, traumatised and ended up treating some of their children as depositories for their split off and projected pain, guilt, shame, and rage. The Mitscherlichs implied in the 1960s that if the German parents in the 1940s and 1950s had been willing to remember the period between 1933 and 1945, and show remorse, all would have been well in their families and institutions. Unfortunately, it was not that simple! They failed to explore the possibility that the perpetrators were experienced by their children as paralysed by guilt and in need of forgetting in order to go on living. The perpetrators could not adequately mourn, the children could not blindly trust. It is clear by now that both perpetrators and their children can only let go of the ghosts of the German dead and victims in a genuine and spontaneous way with the help of re-enactments and a third party as witness. In that sense, the Mitscherlichs' thesis of the inability to mourn is moralistic, as it implies that the failure to show remorse is the result of recalcitrance. What I have found is that Germans need to reclaim their right to mourn their dead, in the eyes of themselves and others, before they can engage in analysis and working through processes. In a similar fashion, Winnicott claimed that patients with very primitive defences can only be analysed when they have felt held by a carer and can engage in play. The Mitscherlichs' "if only" theory redramatises the "failed dependency" the children experienced at the hands of their war traumatised perpetrator parents. It is within this context that the analytic community needs to offer benign leadership to the Germans and try to understand and accept how it is, not how it should be, before engaging in judgement.

References

Bessel, R. (2004). *Nazism and War*. New York: Random House.
Bettelheim, B. (1987). *A Good Enough Parent*. London: Thames & Hudson.
Bohm, D. (2002). *Wholeness and the Implicate Order*. London: Routledge.
Bollas, C. (1991). *Forces of Destiny. Psychoanalysis and the Human Idiom*. London: Free Association Books.
Elias, N. (1991). *Die Gesellschaft der Individuen*. Frankfurt: Suhrkamp
Elias, N. (1992). *Studien über die Deutschen. Machtkämpfe und Habitusentwicklung im 19. und 20. Jahrhundert*. Frankfurt: Suhrkamp
Foulkes, S. H. (1948). *Introduction to Group-analytic Psychotherapy*. London: Heinemann.
Hopper, E. (1991). Encapsulation as a defence against the fear of annihilation. *International Journal of Psychoanalysis, 72*(4): 607–624.
Hopper, E. (1997). Traumatic experiences in the unconscious life of groups: a fourth basic assumption. *Group Analysis, 30*(4): 439–470.
Hopper, E. (2003a). *The Social Unconscious: Selected Papers*. London: Jessica Kingsley.
Hopper, E. (2003b). *Traumatic Experience in the Unconscious Life of Groups*. London: Jessica Kingsley.
Leuzinger-Bohleber, M. (2001). Langzeitwirkungen von Psychoanalysen und Psychotherapien. *Psyche. Zeitschrift für Psychoanalyse und die Anwendungen, 3*: 193–276.
Mitscherlich, A., & Mitscherlich, M. (1967). *Die Unfähigkeit zu trauern. Grundlagen kollektiven Verhaltens*. Munich: Piper.
Niederland, W. G. (1980). *Folgen der Verfolgung: Das Überlebenden-Syndrom, Seelenmord*. Frankfurt: Suhrkamp.
Schmidbauer, W. (1998). *'Ich wusste nie, was mit Vater ist.' Das Trauma des Krieges*. Hamburg: Rowohlt.
Volkan, V. (2002). *The Third Reich in the Unconscious*. New York: Brunner-Routledge.
Wardi, D. (1992). *Memorial Candles: Children of the Holocaust*. London: Routledge.
Wilke, G. (2007). Second generation perpetrator symptoms in groups. *Group Analysis, 40*(4): 429–447.

CHAPTER FIVE

Psychoanalytic view of the totalitarian mentality: the case of the Czech experience

*Olga Marlin**

Introduction

For many years, I have been trying to work through and understand my traumatic experiences growing up under two totalitarian regimes as a child, under Nazi occupation during the Second
World War and, later, under Communist rule in Czechoslovakia. I
turned to psychoanalysis to find answers as to how these developments were at all possible, and why so many people gave up their
rights and freedoms and succumbed to totalitarian rule. As a psychologist, I investigated the psychological causes, taking into account
the many social, economic, and political factors involved in these
developments. In this presentation, I first describe my experiences and
analyses of the totalitarian system in Czechoslovakia in the 1950s and
early 1960s, when totalitarian rule was at its most severe. I then
summarise the ideas of several important psychoanalytic thinkers
about social groups and their application to the analysis of group
processes in the totalitarian regime in Czechoslovakia (Marlin, 1990;
Marlinova, 1998). I conclude by discussing certain attitudes and traits
of Czechs which are rooted in the Czech social unconscious (Hopper,
2003) and associated with their past traumatic experiences.

---

* In the Czech Republic Olga Marlin is known as Olga Marlinova. She has published
under each of these names.

The totalitarian past

Czech society has suffered specific traumas in recent history; the degree of traumatisation varies in different generations. These events, of course, had different psychological impacts on different individuals according to their family histories, social development, personality structures, and political preferences. The focus of this chapter is an exploration of the dynamics of social groups in the totalitarian Communist regime in Czechoslovakia, established in 1948. This chapter concentrates on the development in the Czech region of what was formerly Czechoslovakia. In 1992, Czechoslovakia split into two states—the Czech and Slovak Republics.

In my opinion, there were many causes of the profound national trauma which created a sense of loss, helplessness, and fear of annihilation in Czechs: the experience of the loss of their national integrity (after the Munich Agreement in 1938, which was forced on them by Hitler and signed by France and Britain, when Czechoslovakia had to give up part of its land to Hitler); the loss of the leader (when Czechoslovak President Beneš, following his decision not to fight the German army, resigned and left the country); the experience of abandonment by their allies, which left Czechs shocked, and caused a profound national mourning. Also traumatic was the president's later decision to surrender to the German Army without a fight (despite an efficient mobilisation, the decision was made not to fight). These events, and the subsequent Nazi occupation, were the precursors to domination by Russian and Communist influences.

The traumatic experience of abandonment by their allies and the loss of a leader triggered in the population conscious as well as archaic unconscious fears of annihilation and regressive dynamics. During this time, Czechs felt unprotected by their leaders—they were standing alone in the world against the overwhelming power of a dangerous aggressor. Although an underground resistance developed, it was dissipated after the assassination of the highest-ranking Nazi official in Bohemia, Reinhard Heydrich, by Czech paratroopers in Prague in 1942. Many of its most courageous members were executed or imprisoned by the Nazis, among them many representatives of the Czech elite.

The developments that took place after the war, and later when Communists took over the government, could be viewed psychologically as continuations of these regressive and defensive processes in individuals and groups, and as resulting from past traumas that could not be overcome. In my view, the political and social developments that eventually led to the strong influence of Communist ideology among Czechs were triggered mainly by social defences against feelings of abandonment, humiliation, and fear of annihilation activated by the 1938 Munich Agreement with Hitler, and, later, during the war and the Nazi occupation. These fears increased people's need for protection by a Great Nation that could be relied on. Since president Beneš could not trust the Western allies after they had betrayed him in Munich, during the war he travelled from London to Russia, had talks with Stalin, and signed the agreement of co-operation with the Soviet Union—this despite the many protests of members of his government in exile. President Beneš believed that he could build a bridge between East and West; however, instead, his actions secured the future Soviet domination of Czechoslovakia.

It is significant that after the war, in 1946, the Communist Party received the greatest number of votes in Bohemia (38%). After the Communist coup in 1948, the Czech Communist Party, with the help of Soviets, organised and gradually implemented a totalitarian rule with tight ideological control over its citizens. I propose that in addition to previous war traumas, another significant psychological factor that caused social regression was the repeated loss of "the leader", one who surrendered to an aggressor. Tragically, again in 1948, a very ill President Beneš (who had not recovered from the trauma of Munich), could not stand up to the hard-line Communist pressure and he gave in to their demands despite the protests of democratically minded citizens. Thus, he once again acted as a weak leader (symbolically, as a weak father of the nation) who could not be relied on to protect his people and lead them in a fight against an aggressor. Also, the democratic leaders were not united and strong enough to take decisive action. The Communists had more strength and political influence in the country after 1945, because they were better organised and had worked in close co-operation with the Soviets during and after the war. The Russians at that time enjoyed great popularity as the victors in the war against Nazis and the saviours of the Czech nation. The Communists were able to use this popularity for political propaganda and their eventual putsch against democracy. Although I cannot here give a full historical account of this period, I am attempting to point out the most important events, those that I consider to have had a significant psychological impact on the Czech population.

After the Communist putsch in 1948, citizens' human rights and freedoms were gradually abolished. Everyone was expected to identify with socialism and to work for it. Opposition was severely punished by the Communist government, mainly by illegal methods. Gradually, many democratic politicians, activists, writers, leaders, and members of the Church, as well as leading businessmen, land owners, farmers, and top military officials were persecuted, jailed, executed, or sent to forced labour camps. Between 1948 and 1952, approximately 250,000 people were imprisoned, on average for ten years (often on trumped up charges); some never returned home from prison. Prisoners' families were also persecuted; they lost their homes and properties. Children of political prisoners could not obtain middle- or higher-level education and had to work in low-level jobs. The secret police organised and inflicted sadistic actions against many innocent people because they were democratically minded, socially influential, or wealthy. Many prisoners were tortured in order to extract false confessions from them for crimes against the state. Traditional farmers were also imprisoned or persecuted and their families banned from their villages. They were not even allowed to return to visit family graves. The inflicted terror increased the fear of annihilation in the population, deepened its sense of helplessness, and discouraged any active course; all opposition was severely punished. The Secret police sent provocateurs who incited certain targeted people to become involved in opposition movements or to escape abroad. If they agreed, they were arrested and imprisoned.

In this period, Czech society tragically lost many top members of the intelligentsia, productive businessmen, traditional farmers, and its democratic cultural, political, and military leaders, and members of the Church. The tragic process of the loss of the Czech elite was repeated once again; it had begun during the Nazi occupation when many of the most courageous people who opposed the Nazis ended up executed or sent to concentration camps. Among them were leaders and members of important national civic organisations and religious communities as well as democratic politicians, military leaders, writers, famous artists, and others.

After the Communist putsch in 1948, there was a massive emigration abroad, especially among the intelligentsia and persecuted groups. Political power was held by the Communist Party, and manipulated by Soviet advisers who had ideological control over Czech society, and ordered persecution of the Czech opposition. National history, literature, and science were distorted in accordance with the ideologies of the Czechoslovak and Soviet Communist regimes. Many distinguished Czechs who did not leave the country were executed or imprisoned, and their families had to endure much suffering as well.

Under the Communist regime in Czechoslovakia in the 1950s, censorship was instituted in all areas. Free expression and different points of view were no longer officially permitted; actually, they were looked upon as criminal. People who expressed different views were not tolerated—they became enemies outside of the group. Central to this politically organised process was the restriction of individual choice, freedom, and civil rights of the population. Traditional national organisations, clubs, and associations were forbidden once again, as they had been during the Nazi era. Communist ideology, based on politically approved interpretations of Marx and on the teachings of Lenin and Stalin, was presented and taught in a dogmatic manner and was not to be questioned or criticised (Marlin, 1990).

Psychologically, this totalitarian regime was based on the submission of the individual to the collective, which was led by idealised, omnipotent political leaders. In this regressive process, individuality was suppressed and lost in the forced symbiosis with the group (Fromm, 1941). The whole process was organised and politically controlled by the Communist Party and its members in different levels of the state hierarchy. Children were organised into groups of Pioneers, and young people into Socialist Youth groups. In those times, it was almost impossible for students to avoid membership of these groups because not to be a member meant social exclusion. Party members enjoyed special privileges and held high level jobs in every field and organisation, even though they often lacked the necessary qualifications.

The Communist Party, with its socialist ideology (which had been developing in Czechoslovakia in the pre-war period among workers and also among leftist intelligentsia), initially promised people justice and social welfare. However, it also sanctioned violent means to achieve this goal. After the war, in which many losses and traumas had occurred, many people felt traumatised, helpless, weak, and deprived. This situation created a fertile ground for primitive and regressive feelings and fantasies in individuals and groups. Many people hoped that their needs would be satisfied in a socialist system, which promised to take care of those people who supported it. In addition, socialism was presented in a utopian manner as the most just and giving system of all, in a way that was reminiscent of a fantasy of a new paradise.

I think that the violence sanctioned by Communist ideology was psychologically reinforced by the actual wartime suffering of many people and by an unconscious identification with the aggressor (the Nazis). After the war aggression exploded, as it was now allowed and sanctioned against some people—first of all against the Germans. Unfortunately, President Beneš did not act in accordance with democratic principles when he sanctioned the forceful exclusion of Germans from Czech society and allowed unbridled aggression against them, including violent retributions and scapegoating of the entire group.

Gradually, in the 1950s, other groups of people branded as class enemies were persecuted and excluded from the Czech society as well. Again, scapegoating occurred as a displacement of accumulated aggression. The leaders and ideologists of the Communist Party proclaimed and organised this persecution process, which was led by selected activists and members of the Secret Police. This process had begun after the war, when people branded as collaborators with Germans were persecuted. In many instances, these accusations were misdirected against businessmen and people who had sizable properties, which were then nationalised and, thus, stolen from them. Later, after 1948, despite the Communists' promises to the contrary, not even small shopkeepers could continue with their businesses. Even Czech pilots who had fought heroically against the Germans in the war in Britain were persecuted because they were identified with a Western country that was now viewed ideologically as an enemy. A black and white view of the world prevailed in Communist propaganda. Many promises given by the Party were not kept, and later, during the purges ordered by Stalin, even high-ranking Czech Communists were persecuted, and some were executed. Obviously, no one was safe in this system based on violence, lies, and ideological domination by Party leaders.

To sum up, I have proposed that the traumatisation and abuse suffered by Czechs as a result of the decisions made in Munich and the actions that followed from this pact with Hitler (made by England and France without Czechoslovak involvement), led to social regression which occurred on many levels, in both individuals and in groups. The social regression was further reinforced during the Nazi occupation and the holocaust. After the war and the Nazi occupation, during which Czech society had been abused and traumatised, it was particularly vulnerable because it had not yet recovered from the humiliation, victimisation, and terror suffered in previous years. In this climate, Communist propaganda flourished and appealed to many people who were looking for safety and protection by strong leaders who presented themselves as saviours. Communist ideology thus appealed (consciously and unconsciously) to their dependency needs, soothed their conscious and unconscious fears of abandonment and annihilation, and allowed for a free expression of primitive aggression and rage. It also soothed their helplessness resulting from traumas in the war and the holocaust. Now they were protected by omnipotent leaders against dangers from within and without, as long as they played by given rules. They were promised safety and strength inside a collective and inside the powerful Party.

From a psychoanalytic point of view, although the Communist Party could be looked upon as a symbolic "Big Mother" who protected and supported her "children", they were not permitted any separation from her. The Party required symbiotic fusion and submission. The Communist political leaders could be looked upon as symbolic Big Fathers who knew the right way, who were strong and wise, who set the rules and without whom people would be totally lost. The group as a symbolic "Big Family" allowed for protection and identification with other members. The collective was everything; the individual was nothing. The socialist slogan was "One for all and all for one!" (Marlin, 1990). It was also significant that Communist ideology permitted destructive and sadistic behaviour against its so-called class enemies (or enemies of socialism) with impunity, which allowed scapegoating as an organised way to displace aggression from the most powerful groups in the society (Hopper, 2003). This process resulted also in increased social and interpersonal aggression within Czech society.

However, many Czechs privately held different beliefs and values and they were critical of the regime and the Communist ideology. The memories of the democratic tradition from the First Republic of Czechoslovakia (1918–1928), and of the respected first president, T. G.

Masaryk (a beloved strong father of the nation), who was a prominent social scientist and humanist, remained in people's consciousness and in some families these memories were transmitted to the younger generation. Also, various working groups which were in opposition to Communist ideology gradually developed, although they had to function in unofficial and hidden ways. This progressive development increased in the late 1960s when the grip of the totalitarian regime loosened. At this time, many attempts to find freer creative expression developed, especially in the cultural sphere. This process eventually led to a reform movement in the 1960s, known as the Prague Spring, which was brought to an end by the Soviet invasion in 1968. This was yet another tragic event for Czechs because their country was now occupied by their "Big Friend", the Soviet Union, and their hopes for more freedom were lost once again. Many original members of the Communist Party were expelled because of their participation in the reform movement. As the persecution of people active in the reform movement developed, a massive emigration abroad took place again. Among these emigrants and refugees were many representatives of the Czech intelligentsia, so, tragically, this loss of the Czech elite occurred once again.

Psychoanalytic theories about social groups

The theories of Freud, Bion, Fromm, and Hopper about groups and social systems are relevant to the analysis of totalitarian dynamics as I knew them in Czechoslovakia in the 1950s and early 1960s, as I have described them above. However, I believe that many of these phenomena have occurred in other totalitarian societies as well, and, therefore, my analysis might also be relevant for other regimes.

Freud and group psychology

Freud's ideas about regression in primary groups, in which people give up their ideal and substitute for it the group ideal as embodied in the leader, are highly relevant to totalitarian dynamics. According to Freud, members of the primary group identify with each other and the idealised leader; they have to be equal, and to share with each other the love of the leader who is superior to them (such as in the institution of the Church). Communist ideology became similarly like a new religion. Freud prophetically predicted this development in his work *Group Psychology and the Analysis of the Ego*, (Freud, 1921c). In totalitarian ideology, the illusion was maintained that all members of the group are equal; ideological membership in the Party and other politically led groups were valued above any other type of relationship. Everyone was expected to share in the socialist ideal embodied in the political leaders. Regressive processes in society and in groups were expressed, stimulated, and supported by ideological propaganda, which was omnipresent. Political leaders idealised as symbolic fathers and saviours of mankind were going to lead people to the era of plenty and to the solutions of all our problems. In this "Big Family", everyone had to agree with Communist ideology as the only ultimate Truth. Disobedience was punished by ostracism, imprisonment, and by economic and social sanctions. Although Freud's ideas about regressive family dynamics in primary groups were original and valuable, they could not fully explain all group phenomena in the totalitarian systems that I am describing. In order to find further explanation of totalitarian group phenomena, I turned to the work of W. R. Bion, a prominent representative of English psychoanalysis.

Bion's basic assumptions and society

Bion's ideas about three "basic assumptions" and about a work group as opposed to a basic assumption group are especially relevant for understanding totalitarian dynamics (Bion, 1959). Bion's contention was that the more a group is disturbed, the more central to the group dynamics are the activation of psychotic (infantile) anxiety and defences against it. Bion held that groups are especially prone to the activation of primitive defence characteristics of the paranoid–schizoid and depressive positions, which were described by Melanie Klein. According to Bion, basic assumptions are regressive emotional states in groups that are derived from irrational, unconscious aspects of individuals. They are present in varying degrees in all groups, but more so in disturbed groups. These basic assumptions are increased dependency, fight/flight, and intimate pairing. If these basic assumptions prevail in the group, it resists change and adaptation to reality. The work group on the contrary has realistic goals—this is analogous to the functions of the conscious ego.

Many processes described by Bion are typical of the basic assumption mentality that predominated in the society in the totalitarian system. There were fantasies about omnipotent leaders and dependency on them, as well as the fight/flight mentality. Pervasive primitive defences of splitting and projection occurred in the propaganda and ideology: our group (society) was always seen as good, as opposed to the foreign (capitalistic) society, which was seen as bad. Aggression was projected outside, threat was seen as coming only from enemy states, or enemies of the people within the state, who were critical of the regime and did not want to play by its rules. On the contrary, aggressive acts by political leaders, state officials, and Communist functionaries were denied or rationalised by ideology as right and necessary for the support and defence of socialism. If a person opted publicly for a different or a critical point of view, or wanted or attempted to leave the country, he or she was seen as a traitor and punished by imprisonment or by execution. Messianic ideas were also included in the ideology. Communism was supposed to bring about a perfect society, in which all our needs would be fulfilled and where human problems would no longer exist.

In summary, the official ideology represented mostly the influence of the basic-assumption mentality, while the work group functions were also preserved in the society and continued to maintain development and learning, which influenced some of the society's progress (Marlin, 1990).

From Bion's point of view, Stalin could be seen as a paranoid leader who led the group in a fight/flight. Individual life was not valued; a person was secondary to the preservation of the idealised social group. Bion's ideas about the relationship of the leader and the group are original and illuminating. In contrast to the usual notion of the leader as having special powers, Bion elucidates the dialectic relationship between the group and the leader. The "power" of the leader lies in his ability (pathology) to respond to and articulate the primitive basic assumptions of the group and to become merged with them (Bion, 1959). This fact also explains the "powerful" social influence in the cases of Hitler or Stalin.

Fromm's social unconscious

An important dimension in the analysis of social groups was added by Erich Fromm, a prominent representative of the American Cultural

School. Fromm explored the interplay of unconscious dynamics with the historical and cultural factors that influence them. Following the work of Trigant Burrow (Pertegato & Pertegato, 2013), Fromm used the term "social unconscious". However, he did not expand or clarify its usage in his theory (Hopper & Weinberg, 2011).

Fromm called the ways in which individuals try to escape from the challenges of individuation, freedom, and growth, "mechanisms of escape" (Fromm, 1941). Fromm sees these regressive tendencies as potential driving forces in all people. The irrational methods of an individual relating back to the group are sadomasochism, destructiveness, and automaton-like conformity. Fromm points out that, if the individual finds cultural patterns that satisfy his masochistic striving for symbiosis (such as submission to the leader, or merging with the group in a totalitarian state), he gains illusory security by uniting himself with others who share his feelings. The mechanisms of escape described by Fromm were present in the totalitarian period that I am describing, and they influenced the dynamics of many social groups. Huge political demonstrations were organised which people were forced to attend and to cheer the Communist leaders and the Party. Destructiveness was frequently used against any opposition and against people who were looked upon as potential enemies, as described above. Also, conformity with the ideology was required, since criticism of the political regime and its communist leaders was not officially allowed.

Another important idea of Fromm's is that a dialectic relationship exists between individual neurotic tendencies and cultural patterns. His concept of "social character" helps to explain the influence of cultural patterns on the personality; it is defined as "the essential nucleus of the character structure of most members of a group, which has developed as the result of basic experiences and the mode of life common to that group" (Fromm, 1941). Fromm analyses the authoritarian character typical for the middle class in Germany, which became the psychological base for fascism.

Fromm's description of an authoritarian character corresponded to the common social character in Russia. It could be also frequently found among Czechs (Marlin, 1990). The most important features of an authoritarian character are a craving for submission to a higher power and a conviction that life is not determined by one's own interests and wishes. According to Fromm, it possesses simultaneously sadistic and masochistic traits.

Contemporary contribution of Earl Hopper

Drawing on the work of Fromm, Foulkes, and others who brought sociological ideas to their psychoanalytic understanding of groups, and following Freud and Bion, Hopper developed his theory of the fourth basic assumption: Incohesion: Aggregation/Massification or I:A/M. The fourth basic assumption is a manifestation of a fear of annihilation and its vicissitudes, which are especially intense within groups and social systems that have been traumatised. The author points out that people who have experienced fear of annihilation are likely to form groups that are characterised by "incohesion". Hopper analyses most primitive regressive phenomena in traumatised groups and societies, and elucidates specific feelings and behaviours that occur in them (Hopper, 2003).

Hopper's ideas further elucidate many psychological phenomena in totalitarian systems. The fourth basic assumption could be seen in totalitarian societies as manifest in various social and group phenomena. Czech society was repeatedly traumatised, as I have described, and regressive group psychological dynamics developed in response to the fear of annihilation and fear of abandonment, as well as in response to a failed dependency. Clearly, the hysterical idealisation of the group and the leader, identification with him and with the group itself, were the central dynamics that led to pseudo-morale and illusions of well-being. Mass spectacles were also common ways of expressing and stimulating a sense of symbiotic fusion with the group, and submission to idealised leaders. Hopper points out that groups characterised by aggregation and massification often use impersonal ways of communication like bureaucracies, and dominant and exclusive use of one official language. This description fits totalitarian ideology and propaganda with its pseudo-scientific approach. Hopper also discusses patterns of aggression in regressed social systems as characterised by incohesion ranging from moral corruption, to character assassination, and actual assassination. As I have pointed out, moral corruption and character assassination occurred frequently in political and social groups in the totalitarian period, even within the group of Communist party members. This process created and reinforced fear of authority and the system, which was destructive to individual integrity and human dignity, and forced people into helplessness and compliance with the regime.

Czech attitudes and character traits
reflecting totalitarian experience

In the totalitarian period that I am describing, hidden opposition was often expressed as avoidance; critical political views could be shared only within a family or with a few trusted friends. Upon my return to the Czech Republic in 1994, and during my subsequent work at the university, I observed an avoidant stance still to be common, especially among the older and middle-aged generations. I was often told by my colleagues that something which was new could not be done: new projects or changes were not welcomed. In the past, people had learnt that being inexpressive or passive was a safe way to be. It could be described as learnt helplessness. They had to turn their aggression and anger in social situations mostly inward, which, in turn, reinforced their passive–aggressive attitudes. Another way in which the past still influences Czechs is in their fear of authorities, and in their submissive behaviour toward them. Czechs in the older and middle generations often do not question official decisions, such as doctors' or teachers' judgements. In the past, teachers, doctors, and nurses as well as bureaucrats were often authoritarian, rude, and punitive. This behaviour is often present still today among generations of professionals who grew up during the totalitarian period. Traditionally, children were often treated in an authoritarian way in Czech families; physical punishment was commonly used as a disciplinary measure. Shaming was used as a guidance method in families and also by teachers in schools. In graduate classes in psychology that I taught at Charles University from 1995–2000, I found that most students were afraid to speak up and express critical opinions, despite my encouragement. Since independent thinking had usually been discouraged in their previous schooling experience, they learnt to remain silent and to agree with the teacher. Generally, assertive behaviour has been traditionally discouraged in Czech children and also in women, who often remained in submissive relationships towards men. Women often viewed men as a higher authority, admired them uncritically, and remained dependent on them despite their own competence. Women who were assertive were often criticised as masculine. I experienced this attitude when I offered my help to a committee of the Psychological Society, and I was told by a woman colleague that I should wait with my proposals until I was asked. I also found that teamwork was rare and that established ways of teaching were given preference and support.

After my return from America, where I had experienced being encouraged in my proposals in psychoanalytic institutes in New York, I continued to express initiative at the university even though this behaviour was often met with negative or avoidant reactions from my colleagues and superiors. Gradually, I learnt that some professional groups functioned as closed groups, including the Czech Psychoanalytic Society. Despite the interest I expressed in activities of the society, I was not invited to participate there or even to hear invited professional speakers from abroad. Contrary to my experiences in America, psychoanalysis was, by some, treated then as a secret field that brought power and financial privilege, not as important knowledge to be shared with others. In this way, an unfortunate development that had taken place in the past in America among Freudians was repeated here. Interestingly, this was not the case with the Czech Psychotherapy Association, which was run as an open and a democratic group, one which welcomed my contribution.

In my opinion, functioning as a closed group was necessary and a safer way of functioning during the totalitarian past. However, afterwards, this functioning was blocking further development in the field. The exclusion of other people who were different—"not one of us"— functioned as a social defence in order to preserve the "unity" and the power of the group and its leaders.

Summary

In order to function within the totalitarian system, people had to sacrifice vital areas of autonomy which often resulted in fear, learnt helplessness, and in suppression of assertiveness, initiative, and responsibility. Aggression was mostly turned inward or projected to other people and groups. Public and private personas were often split. Moral relativism, alienation, irresponsibility, clientelism, and corruption mostly developed in the Czech society during and after the Second World War and during the totalitarian period. Unfortunately, after the Soviet occupation of 1968, during the period called "normalisation" (which was actually highly abnormal), people once again had to live under a corrupt regime, one supported by the Soviet government. Gradually, this regime became more and more dysfunctional. In the late 1970s, a democratic group developed, called Charter 77, that connected people of different political backgrounds in their fight for human rights. This initiative and other unofficial activities such as underground cultural performances, scientific seminars, civic interest groups, and working groups preserved a cultural continuity with Czech national history and with the world at large. Their leaders and members eventually became civic and political activists who worked for change, which led to the peaceful demise of the Communist regime in 1989, with the support of the majority of the population (Marlin & Smith, 1991).

Now, after twenty years of democratic rule in Czech society, many old attitudes are still rooted in individuals, official institutions, groups, and political parties. Many Czechs (especially those from older generations) are still suspicious of "different others". They prefer old connections and closed social and professional groups. They do not trust their political representatives, whose corrupt behaviour often goes unpunished. People complain and criticise the wrongdoings of officials; however, many have not been active in political and civic protests because they feel that they cannot influence the functioning of their government or their leaders. Gradually, however, more people are joining community organisations and civic groups and staging political protests and happenings. Many people among the younger generations are more open, cosmopolitan, and politically active. It is to be hoped that their activities in civic organisations and in politics will eventually lead to positive changes in Czech society.

References

Bion, W. R. (1959). *Experience in Groups.* New York: Ballantine.

Freud, S. (1921c). *Group Psychology and the Analysis of the Ego. S. E., 18*: 67–143. London: Hogarth.

Fromm, E. (1941). *Escape from Freedom.* New York: Holt, Rinehart, and Winston.

Hopper, E. (2003). *Traumatic Experience in the Unconscious Life of Groups.* London: Jessica Kingsley.

Hopper, E., & Weinberg, H (Eds.) (2011). *The Social Unconscious in Persons, Groups and Societies, Volume.* London: Karnac.

Marlin, O. (1990). Group psychology in the totalitarian system. *Group*, *14*(1): 44–58.

Marlin, O., & Smith, N. (1991). Bridging East and West, in politics and psychology. In: J. Offerman-Zuckerberg (Ed.), *Politics and Psychology, Contemporary Psychodynamic Perspectives* (pp. 207–228). New York: Plenum.

Marlinova, O. (1998). *Psychoanalytický rozbor totalitní mentality* [Psychoanalytic View of the Totalitarian Mentality]. Psychoterapie VI, Prague: Triton.

Pertegato, E., & Pertegato, G. (Eds.) (2013). *From Psychoanalysis to Group Analysis: The Pioneering Work of Trigant Burrow*. London: Karnac.

CHAPTER SIX

Contemporary manifestations of the social unconscious in Japan: post trauma massification and difficulties in identity formation after the Second World War*

Kaoru Nishimura

Japan has suffered massive social trauma and the Japanese people continue to work through their distress using various coping mechanisms. The social unconscious (Hopper, 2003a, 2012; Hopper & Weinberg, 2011; Weinberg, 2007) is a concept that helps us shed light on this process. Social reactions to trauma include the basic assumption of Incohesion: Aggregation/Massification (Hopper, 2003b), the various forms of instrumental adjustments (Hopper, 1981), and other socially patterned defensive processes (Hopper & Weinberg, 2011). Trauma can touch an entire society, destabilising the sense of identity of an entire nation, including the self-identity of citizens.

The major trauma of defeat in the Second World War left the people of Japan with a profound internal conflict around their national identity. The issue of war trauma was hardly addressed in the public discourse. Elements of popular culture, including *Space Battleship Yamato* and other films emerged as a medium for the expression of such trauma, hving a great impact on subsequent generations.

---

* This is a modified version of the paper "Unresolved trauma seen in the Japanese identity after the Second World War" in *Forum* (Nishimura, 2010). The first version was presented to the IAGP Conference in Rome, August 2009.

The untreated and unelaborated trauma of the Second World War had a strong impact on reactions to the most terrifying destruction Japan would later face in the 3/11 (2011) disasters, the combination of earthquake, tsunami, and nuclear plant meltdown.

Historical comments and national identity of modern Japan

Japan is sometimes seen only as an island nation with a unique culture. However, since ancient times, Japan has always borrowed from "advanced" civilisations; for example, from the seventh century, Japan's political elite actively imported political and administrative systems, literature, religion, ideas, and technology from the Chinese mainland. The concept of *wakon kansai* (blending Chinese knowledge with the Japanese spirit) was born in Japan's medieval period. The spirit of being Japanese people (*yamato damashii*), as opposed to being Chinese or foreign, gradually became a key term in Japanese identity formation. In this way, Japan skilfully created a national identity, but underneath remained a fundamental anxiety.

Historically, Japan has experienced a series of fateful crises. They arguably constitute parts of "chosen trauma" (Volkan, 2001). For example, with the Mongol Invasions (1274, 1281), what is important to the Japanese social unconscious is that when a great storm destroyed the Mongolian fleet (second Mongol Invasion), it was believed that the storm winds were blown by the gods to protect the nation. Thus, the winds were named *kamikaze* (the wind of gods). The famous Kamikaze attacks in the Second World War were so named in the expectation of invoking similar divine protection.

At the end of the Warring States Period (mid-fifteenth century to the mid-sixteenth century), warlords who succeeded in unifying the nation sought the emperor's authority to govern. In times of crisis involving threats to Japan's national survival and national identity, emperors acted as a kind of socio-cultural "glue" that helped to connect the people when they were about to lose social cohesion, a symbol with which the people can feel oneness through narcissistic identification (Pines, 2003). This was in contrast to times of peace and stability when the emperors were ignored.

In 1853, the American naval officer Perry arrived in Japan, demanding a treaty of commerce that would open Japan to the world.

The Edo shogunate was forced to give in to this pressure and, after fifteen years of national debate and civil war, was replaced in 1868 by a "restoration" of imperial rule. The new government, centralised under the imperial symbol, pursued rapid westernisation while constructing a new national identity. This is similar to what happened earlier with Japan's encounter with China. That is, Japan tried to make itself look equal to the other advanced countries and, at the same time, forge a unity from within. The emperor was used again to serve as symbolic glue, and a governing structure based on an emperor was created.

The concept *wakon yosai* (blending western knowledge with the Japanese spirit) was used to explain Japan's westernisation. In effect, this was a modern version of *wakon kansai*. As a result of Japan's wealth and power policies (*fukoku kyohei*), the nation was able to win the Japanese–Sino War and the Japanese–Russo War. Later, due to social and economic problems at home and conflict with the USA, Japan entered the Second World War, joining Germany and Italy in a tripartite alliance. Once again the phrase *yamato damashii* became a nationalistic slogan, urging Japanese to fight for their country and for their emperor.

People were educated from primary school to serve the emperor and to sacrifice themselves for the sake of the nation. Nationalism was encouraged and strengthened through *bushido*, the ethical code of the samurai warriors. This antique value system was creatively used (some would say distorted) by Japan's military leaders in the 1930s in order to valorise both the fighting skills and martial spirit of Japan's military forces, but also to celebrate values such as loyalty, honour, and courage in the general public. This ethical code was purified and reinforced through education in a process that amounted to indoctrination. The danger of reinforcing *bushido* was that it promoted a climate in which suicide became acceptable, for complete self-sacrifice was seen as a virtue. Being captured meant shame; suicidal attack, on the other hand, was a heroic act.

These social dynamics may be described by Hopper's theory of the fourth basic assumption incohesion: aggregation/massification. As he says, ". . . in massified societies, the regulation of aggression can be seen in various forms of nationalism, which are associated with the purification of language, race, ethnicity, custom and even aesthetic values" (2003b, p. 76). "The pressures to conform and to comply are immense. The boundaries of a group are marked continuously, and personal identity is asserted in terms of membership of the group" (2003b, p. 77).

If someone did not conform to the ethical code they "lost face", were seen as *hikokumin* (a traitor or unpatriotic person), and were forced to punish themselves. It was a terrible pressure that forced people to comply with society's norms, such that *seppuku*, or *hara-kiri*, ritual suicide by self-disembowelment, became the ultimate test of loyalty and courage of the twentieth-century warrior. Therefore, even if one were to refuse to participate in a suicidal attack, death would follow none the less. Hopper noted,

> Aggressive feelings and aggression become more essential to the maintenance of massification . . . To anonymise a person is to destroy his identity as a unique person. Anonymisation reduces the sense of personal responsibility for thought, feeling and deed. (Hopper, 2003b, pp. 77–78)

After the Second World War, occupation leaders, including General Douglas MacArthur, understood that the Japanese were afraid that their identity might cease to exist if the imperial family was removed from the world of politics. Douglas chose to maintain the emperor system in the construction of a new democratic political system as a way to ensure that the occupation reforms would proceed smoothly. In this way, the emperor was used again as a symbol to unify the nation.

Japan's social structure was able to adapt to change by replacing one central idea or symbol for unification with another. In this case, change was quickly brought about by changing the emperor from god to human being, defined in Japan's new constitution as the "symbol of the unity of the Japanese people" and operating in such a way as to enhance Japan's new commitment to peace and democracy. However, this itself caused another identity confusion.

Defeat forced the Japanese people to question the meaning of their lives. Some, with the terrible experience of watching their family and fellow soldiers die, suffered from survivor's guilt. All in all, Japanese people felt a strong sense of shame that they had been defeated. Many Japanese people felt that they had lost an important part of their identity, and were consumed by feelings of emptiness and isolation. These post-war reactions created aspects of a social system characterised by aggregation. It was considered taboo for individuals to speak of their torment (moreover, criticism of the USA was censored by occupation authorities).

The deleterious effects of such identity confusion continue even today. For example, some teachers to this day express reluctance to fly the national flag or sing the national anthem during school cere-monies. They know that the national anthem (the *Kimigayo*) celebrates the glory of the imperial family, and, above all, that it is associated with wartime. It is more common for Japanese people to have vague feelings of shame and guilt about their nationality. Moreover, Japan's neighbours in Asia, many of which were former objects of Japanese aggression, continue to condemn Japan and the Japanese. In some cases, they even distort historical truth, because they are, at the same time, unable to resolve their own traumas. Japan has oscillated between open liberalism and ultra-nationalism. Opinion is sharply divided on whether to accept blame and apologise, or somehow attempt to justify Japan's military actions in Asia. As a result, the Japanese government has apologised several times, but subsequent actions and statements by conservative politicians have often under-mined the sincerity of those apologies. A part of this is isomorphic to the relationship with the USA. While the two countries have an actual, co-operative relationship, at the same time there is a smouldering resentment within Japan towards America's use of nuclear weapons and the massacre that they caused. The USA also oscillates between recognising their wrongdoing and justifying it.

Japanese foundation matrix

Nakane (1973), a social anthropologist, wrote that Japanese society is a vertical society marked by a strong ranking-consciousness in a homogeneous society. Even forty years after its publication, Nakane's theory remains perceptive in describing Japanese social structure.

According to Nakane, a Japanese group's functioning power depends on emotional relationships established on a personal level. In Japan, a sense of oneness tends to be emphasised, so the group members do not raise objections or counter-arguments that others might find unfavourable for fear of becoming isolated from the group.

Individuals, therefore, become sensitive to the group atmosphere. Such an emotional sense of oneness is a significant interpersonal incentive in Japan's foundation matrix (Foulkes, 1973).

In this kind of social structure in Japan, feelings of loyalty among the members accelerate, often producing self-sacrificing behaviour. Because the group acts are based on emotional rather than fundamental principles, it is easy for the group to lose logical thinking and weaken its commitment to justice, at times leading to irrational and implausible decisions, particularly in situations of crisis and conflict. Dissatisfaction with unanimous agreements might, in fact, lead to more extreme self-sacrificing behaviour as a sort of reaction formation.

There are many historical figures who were defeated but, none the less, are considered heroes: for example, Minamoto no Yoshitsune, the forty-seven ronin, Takamori Saigo, and members of the Shinsengumi. These are people who, in the end, died fighting with resentment. In a way, their loyalty brought on tragedy. This is something many Japanese inwardly fear, but, at the same time, romanticise. Doi (1973) writes concerning Japanese resentment that it is cathartic for people to remember stories of those thought also to have suffered the chagrin of defeat. From a contemporary Jungian perspective, this might well be referred to as a "cultural complex" (Singer & Kimbles, 2004).

Repetition of trauma after the war: unconscious processes in society and popular culture

After the Second World War, the public welcomed westernisation, the introduction of democracy, and American support. That industrialisation progressed and the economy rapidly grew is well known. There was an unconscious driving force behind Japan's rush to recover from the war. It can be understood as a defence mechanism that allowed people to escape agony and leave it unspoken.

Then aggregation threatened to emerge: having high demands for becoming one with a group and presenting massification in the face of external threat (and, when that collapses, installing a new idea or symbol at the centre), these processes comprise manifesting pattern of the social unconscious that is repeated in Japan. Moreover, the group's victims represent the public's experience of being eventually betrayed by the group to which they had expressed loyalty, leading to the worship of popular tragic heroes.

Feelings of resentment and chagrin, which are still not completely dissolved, can be expressed through various cultural means. Popular culture allows for free expression of these feelings through the use of fantastic metaphors. An important example is the animated television series *Space Battleship Yamato*. It was broadcast in Japan in 1974 and later in many other countries, including the USA. This story is based on the real Battleship *Yamato* of the Imperial Japanese Navy (IJN). In the animated version, *Space Battleship Yamato* fights against, and finally saves, the earth and humankind from aliens that threaten the earth with radioactive bombs that bring the earth to the verge of ruin.

Needless to say, the story is derived from the real history of the IJN Battleship *Yamato* and symbolically revives the trauma of war. The *Yamato* was the largest and strongest battleship in the world at that time and served as the symbol of Japanese military, technology, and industry, as well as of the country itself. In the Second World War, where air battles became more important, the *Yamato* and its sister ship *Musashi* became redundant (the *Yamato* was commissioned in late 1941, just after the air attack on Pearl Harbor). In 1945, having lost command of the air, it was obvious to Japan that were the navy to send the *Yamato* and the other battleships, they would all be sunk. Japan was, therefore, not able to carry out naval operations. However, a dilemma presented itself in the spring of 1945: Japan could not just leave the "symbol of the navy" and idly watch the American forces attack Okinawa. The navy's only available strategy was to send the great battleship to Okinawa without air defence. On the way there, on 7 April 1945, the battleship was attacked by hundreds of warplanes and sunk. In this way, the *Yamato* became a symbol of chagrin and its story continued to live in the minds of people long after the event. There are many films and documentaries related to it, and the Yamato Museum, opened in 2005, has a huge model of the battleship.

Space Battleship Yamato is an example of what de Mendelssohn might call a "heroic-solution" attempt. "'[H]eroic solution' to the problem of shame, daring to be proud of what was once considered shameful has its positive functions, since it attempts to restore those ego functions that have been damaged by shameful experience" (de Mendelssohn, 2008, p. 399).

Space Battleship Yamato, produced twenty-eight years after the sinking of the IJN *Yamato*, embodies the original "heroic" story. The scene where the battleship leaves the earth as a spaceship reminds people of the original charge to Okinawa. Needless to say, the radioactive bombs possessed by the aliens remind us of the atomic bombs dropped on Hiroshima and Nagasaki. The arrival of "Radiation Removal Equipment" suggests how the Japanese people have a deep wish to be freed from nuclear threats. Interestingly, even in the new story, the entire crew is Japanese. The fact that they were united in their effort to save the earth might be the best and most constructive way ever to repay old scores. Here, too, lies the spirit of self-sacrifice. It is emphasised that *Space Battleship Yamato*'s Captain Okita died right before returning to the earth, saving the planet in exchange for his life.

One of the reasons that *Space Battleship Yamato* became popular in the 1970s was that Japan was being entangled in the oil shock brought about by the 1973 war in the Middle East. In Japan, people were overwhelmed by sudden rise in the price of oil, which led to a general rise in commodity prices. People panicked and rushed to supermarkets, competing with each other to buy things. Japan became hugely anxious about its future. As a reflection of this dismal social atmosphere, occult groups and Nostradamus' prophecies began to boom. A shocking film, *Japan Sinking* (1973), swept Japan. Interest in apocalyptic themes prevailed.

The social reactions during the period of the oil shock recapitulated the fear of the early post-war days of devastation and hunger. For children, the adults' panic looked like a terrible threat: it not only evoked excessive anxiety about the future, as if it really was at the end of the world, but conveyed the original fear and trauma of war.

An older popular artistic work that conveys the trauma of the tragedy of Japan is *Godzilla*. The first *Godzilla* film came out in 1954. It conveyed the vivid experiences of the war and the audience identified with people in the film who were wounded and desperate for help. A monster appeared from the bottom of the ocean after nuclear tests, burning Tokyo, destroying myriad buildings, including the Diet Building, and terrorising people.

The *Godzilla* film was made in the wake of the fishing boats, including *Daigo Fukuryu Maru*, being exposed to nuclear fallout from an American H-bomb test in Bikini Atoll. Godzilla himself was covered with skin that has been burned black by H-bombs. Thus, the film involves a strong protest against the new nuclear age. That is, the first Godzilla represented the fear of H-bombs, a current fear (1954) overlapped with past trauma (1945).

After *Godzilla*, a number of films were made with the motif of contamination by nuclear testing or nuclear war. These films also represent the horror and anger evoked in people at that time by the nuclear tests in the South Pacific. A Japanese sociologist, Yoshii (2008), analysed the series of monster films that used special effects, starting with *Godzilla*, to show how the Japanese people felt threatened by nuclear testing.

There is another work that directly portrayed the harsh reality of nuclear warfare: *Barefoot Gen*, a comic. It came out in 1973, one year before *Space Battleship Yamato*. This story is based on the author, Keiji Nakazawa's, own experience. His family members died as a result of the A-bomb explosion in Hiroshima, except for his mother. Twenty-one years later, his mother died and left not even one piece of her bones after she was cremated.[1] Radiation had eaten into her body. Enraged, Nakazawa decided to make this comic. This unusual release in a comic for young people left a strong impact on its youthful readers. The horrific scenes from the explosion, the dead bodies, the dying people, mothers looking like ghosts with their babies on their backs, and the destroyed towns are explicit and dreadful. The comic describes very clearly and honestly the oppression of the military and the prejudice people have, the stigma of the *Hibakusha*, those who were affected by the A-bombs. Nowadays, most schools have this series in the library and most children have read it at least once. It has been featured as a series of films (1976, 1977, 1980), animated films (1983, 1986), and as a television drama (2007). Because of its realistic content, it has left a strong impression on children.

In essence, however developed a society may be, the experience of massive trauma embedded these traumatic memories into the social unconscious of its citizens, reviving fear and creating panic when new social anxieties are experienced. Volkan (2002) referred to this condition as the "societal regression". Not only do various works become mediums for sharing that fear within society through images and narratives, but they also act as a sociocultural transmission to following generations.[2]

In contrast, figures such as "heroes with chagrin" and "tragic heroes", who try to protect society and nation by self-sacrifice—an inheritance of Japan's foundation matrix—have been created in many works. Imaginary heroic solutions are seen in some of them; however, in these instances, the cultural icon is easily dissociated from the original traumatic experience, sequels usually turning into something harmless. The traumatic memories are then harboured in the social unconscious. On the other hand, personal experience directly conveys real traumatic memories.

My personal experience: implicit transmission of trauma in my family

I belong to a generation that, as a child, watched news of the Vietnam War and of Japan's Student Movement and experienced the panic caused by the oil shock. During my childhood, my parents were extremely busy trying to make money as they managed a small franchise shop. My father worked until midnight every day and took only a few days off a year. My mother helped in the shop and was almost as busy. My father rarely talked to me and never about his experiences in the wartime. I had guessed that he had lost his father early and that he did not think well of his mother, but he never brought these things up. Instead I learnt about him through my mother. She once told me that the Tokyo air raids killed my father's father. I believed in her story for a long time.

The group atmosphere of the franchise company emphasised sales performance and created slogans that were humiliating for the shop owner, such as "You are a *gusano*! Swallow your pride." It was believed that pride would make them conceited. It was clearly a group with aspects of massification. The same people who rejected loyalty to the nation after the war were unconsciously repeating the pattern they hated. Economic growth after the war was achieved rapidly by organisations demanding obedience like that. Thus, the dynamics of a larger social system is recapitulated in a subsystem (Hopper, 2003b; Hopper & Weinberg, 2011; Nuttman-Shwartz & Weinberg, 2012).

These massified organisations demanded so much from their workers that they valued loyalty to the company before their families. For this reason, the children of these families were neglected. Traumatic reaction to the wartime was another reason for this neglect. Hardship, my parents firmly believed, was created by a sense of despair without food and money in a devastated atmosphere such as they had experienced during and after the war. Thus, no one in my family could respond psychologically to my needs.

It was in those days that the oil shock occurred and Nostradamus' prophesies and *Space Battleship Yamato* became popular. I felt unprotected and neglected by my family and by society. It was really difficult for children like me to trust the society. Many of us did not have the good fortune of being taught how to master anxieties in real life. For us, "virtual" salvation in those special effects hero dramas and films had a greater influence.

I despised secular needs, hated the world, and turned my interests to inner concerns. From the social unconscious viewpoint, it may be considered that neglect within the family was brought about by self-sacrificial labour as a defence against having to deal with the encapsulated pessimism from war, and then parents transferred their pessimism to their children.

In the 1980s, Japanese society was bubbling; people identified self-actualisation with selfishness and economic success. After I was admitted to university, I started to live on my own and entered a Buddhist religious cult. It was different from antisocial cults such as AUM Shinrikyo (described later), but, as most cults are, this group was also massified. The idea of reincarnation that wrong deeds lead to hell and daily spiritual practices lead to salvation worked as a terrible threat that confined individuals and absorbed individual human values into the principles of the group.

Although I decided to drop out after several months, it was ironic that I became involved with a massified group after escaping from my father's grasp. But this is the transgenerational transmission of trauma: the same pattern is repeated by the parent and the child. I and others of my generation had trouble establishing our identity, repeating as we did so often the unelaborated and unspoken trauma of war that took place before we were born.

After my father retired, he tried to discover his roots and decided to write an autobiographic essay, telling me a lot about the wartime and his family history. After his parents' divorce in 1940, he lived with his father and grandmother. In 1941, when he was seven, his father died of a sudden sickness in a small factory where he had started a new business one month after the attack on Pearl Harbor. Three years later, my father lost his grandmother. Finally, he decided to live with his mother, who had not seen him for a long time and by then was living with another man. After he and his younger brother survived several air raids in a big city, they moved to a rural town. After the war, a time when there were few goods, while studying at middle school, my father helped his mother earn money to support the family as his stepfather had no income.

Numerous homes were ruined due to war. What can be seen in this account is a man (my grandfather) who died—much to his chagrin—without being able to protect his family, a man (my father) who sacrificed himself and worked to protect his family on behalf of his father, bearing a grudge against the war. Stories of Japan's recovery after the war are often told, but it is difficult for individuals with a "psychic hole" (Gampel & Mazor, 2004) to show the meaning of life to their families. Rather than by working, but by putting into words his war experiences, did my father fill his psychic hole, teaching me the reason for my own feelings of emptiness, and deepening the meaning of my life.

AUM Shinrikyo: a terrorist cult as a collectivistic personification of the social unconscious of Japan

In the 1990s, several religious cults arose in Japan. The most famous among them was AUM Shinrikyo. It started as a training organisation for yoga practice, becoming a religious corporation under its charismatic leader, Shoko Asahara. Later, it became militarised, attacking the government and the general population and finally carrying out a large-scale terrorist sarin gas attack on the Tokyo subway in 1995.

Haruki Murakami, a well-known Japanese novelist, became strongly interested in that attack. He interviewed victims and published a book titled *Underground* (2001[1997]), and followed it with *In the place that was promised: Underground Two* (2001[1998]) that included interviews with believers and ex-believers of AUM Shinrikyo. These interviews revealed that most of these people had suffered from mental crises, including isolation from family and peer groups. They were more or less self-reflective, although they tended to be self-righteous, world-weary, and pessimistic, having contempt for secular success and a hunger for a clear perspective of the world. It is easily recognisable that their accounts are similar to my own experiences, as I mentioned above. Murakami (2001[1998]) concluded that the AUM Shinrikyo cult members had lost their own way of individual thinking, abandoning themselves to dogma. However, we must remember that they had already been socially isolated. They had not formed their identity based on values shared by the society. In fact, after initiation into AUM, even though members lived together in the same facility, there was not much communication between them. Each was concentrating on his or her practices. They sought a charismatic saviour because of their sense of isolation, which is how the group was formed. The group was, therefore, in a state of aggregation. This was a group of traumatised people who had both aspects of aggregation and massification, oscillating between the two.

The leader, Shoko Asahara, had an unfortunate childhood. He was obsessed with his grandiose self and notions of self-salvation. As AUM Shinrikyo began to militarise, while regarding American and Jewish people with hostility, they developed delusions that they would free the world. This is a pathological salvation wish but actually a recapitulation of the ideals held by the Imperial Japanese Army. That is, Asahara and AUM are personifications of what the Japanese people harboured in their social unconscious after the war. The wish among those who became isolated from society to be rescued was absorbed, thereby encouraging the organisation to develop.

Interestingly, the AUM Shinrikyo sometimes adopted images from *Space Battleship Yamato*. While producing poisonous gas inside the sect's facilities, leader Asahara was under the delusion that he was being attacked with gas. He installed an air purification system inside their facilities. This device, called the *Cosmo-cleaner*, developed by the AUM technicians, was named after the Radiation Removal Equipment that appeared in *Space Battleship Yamato*. During his early adolescence, Asahara was been strongly drawn to the heroic rescue depicted in the story. An ex-AUM executive of my generation (Joyu, 2012) wrote that he had also been strongly influenced by *Space Battleship Yamato* when he was confronted with the Nostradamus boom and a sense of helplessness as a result of the oil shocks. *Space Battleship Yamato* appealed to children by giving them a heroic fantasy to cling to. If *Space Battleship Yamato* is the second coming of the Japanese army, made to clear away the chagrin and resentment left within Japan's social unconscious, we can argue then that AUM was an organisation that attempted through pseudo-religious and delusional means to resolve these untreated social wounds and the sense of isolation that was present after the war. AUM Shinrikyo dissolved and many former believers have been de-brainwashed, but successors have established

"Aleph", an organisation still active to this day which is actively recruiting new believers.

Aspects of social unconscious in the aftermath of the Great East Japan earthquake

Japan Sinking grabbed the undivided attention of people when it came out in 1973. Japan has a realistic reason to be afraid of apocalypse: that is, earthquakes. Japan, lying at the edge of a tectonic plate that leads to trenches in the Pacific Ocean, is an earthquake-prone country that has met, and will continue to experience, extremely powerful earthquakes. People in Japan cannot help living their daily life in denial of this incredible fact to a greater or lesser extent. Most Japanese people anticipated that a huge quake would take place around the Tokai area.

On 11 March 2011, a huge earthquake (M 9.0) with numerous aftershocks and a massive tsunami struck the Tohoku area, the most powerful earthquake recorded in Japanese history, claiming almost 16,000 lives and leaving about 2,700 missing (as of December, 2013). Many coastal communities were wiped out, forcing more than 10,000 people to take shelter in evacuation centres. Moreover, the accidents of the Fukushima Daiichi Nuclear Plant caused widespread discharge of radioactive materials, affecting a wider area than the tsunami.

Certainly, this earthquake reminded many people of the unique "chosen trauma" of their social unconscious (Weinberg, 2007): the 1995 Great Hanshin-Awaji Earthquake and the 1923 Great Kanto Earthquake. The tsunami victims also referred to huge tsunamis after earthquakes in 1896 and 1933. In addition, the destruction of villages and towns, many reduced to rubble, reminded people of the destruction wrought by wartime air raids and A-bombs. When the roads were cut off and transport of goods fell behind, people rushed to the stores to buy necessary fuel, batteries, beverages, and even toilet paper. This is a clear relapse of the panic that accompanied the oil shock in 1974.

More important is how the Japanese people, who repeatedly experienced feelings of chagrin and resentment, were able to cope with the feelings that resulted from this natural disaster. The term *mujo* (a Buddhist concept of impermanence) played a role. It is rooted in Japan's foundation matrix, and functions as a defence against hopelessness, guilt, or aggregation, and, to some extent, is helpful in overcoming such hardships. Freud (1916a) wrote about "transience" in relation to the individual's mourning, but, in Japan, *mujo* serves more as a socially established cultural pattern.

In his acceptance speech at the Catalunya International Prize on 10 June 2011, Haruki Murakami used this concept to describe the way Japanese people think of natural disasters:

> I think being Japanese means living with disasters . . .This view of the world was derived from Buddhism, but the idea of *mujo* was burned into the spirit of Japanese people beyond the strictly religious context, taking root in the common ethnic consciousness from ancient times. . . . I'm sure . . . that in some sense we have been able to collectively overcome successive natural disasters and to accept the unavoidable by virtue of this mentality.

The concept of *mujo* helps to accept an unchangeable reality.

Encouraging phrases such as *Gambaro!* [Let's hang on patiently and do our best] and words such as *kizuna* [bond] are valued and widely used. People soon began to recognise that what has befallen them is somehow fated, perhaps fated to them as Japanese. This philosophy of resignation might also be seen as part of survivor's guilt: even those living in the most devastated areas regarded their torment as being less than that of their neighbours, which is why many victims did not speak about their troubles. This may be recognised as a form of social masochism. It seems that the spirit of self-sacrifice found in Japan's foundation matrix was present before *bushido* was invented, that it was born much earlier out of repeated experiences of loss from past natural disasters.

Each victim was, thus, isolated. Although disaster-struck areas produced a state of aggregation, enduring loss and working silently has become something of a recognised aesthetic. People outside of the devastated areas tended to refrain from indulging in pleasure. The governor of Tokyo commented soon after the disaster, "We need to make use of this tsunami and wash away the selfish desires of Japanese people. I believe the tsunami was a punishment from heaven." For this he was severely criticised and forced to apologise. Thus, the entire society was in a state of massification.

As society's interests begin to fade over time, there is an increase in the sense of isolation in the devastated areas and between the victims. On the other hand, in the same speech, Murakami noted that people in Japan should have been unrelenting in saying "No" to nuclear power. He must have spoken these words on behalf of many Japanese people and their grief. It was estimated, as of November 2013, that Fukushima Prefecture lost some 78,000 of its population in two and a half years, over 1,600 of who were dead due to disaster-related reasons (e. g., physical and mental fatigue from living in evacuation centres, worsening of pre-existing illness, suicide).

If we take into consideration the severe trauma from defeat in war and radiation exposure, it seems strange that Japanese people allowed and even encouraged the construction and maintenance of nuclear plants throughout the country. In 1954, when Japan faced repeated instances of nuclear contamination, the government lobbied for monies for research and development of atomic energy under the pretext of "peaceful utilisation of nuclear energy". Against the opposition of many citizens, but with the full support of the USA, the government decided to build Japan's first atomic power plant (which went into operation in 1963). In fact, many municipal governments sought to build nuclear energy plants, hoping to stimulate industrial development.

There was self-deceit in this process. Promoting economic development under the pretext of "peaceful utilisation of nuclear energy" conveniently concealed the trauma of war and the A-bombs. Somewhere along the line, it seems as if the whole of Japanese society came to deny the threat of nuclear plants, pushing these fears into the social unconscious. Having lost the war, Japan tried to recover its lost pride by developing nuclear plants and becoming an advanced country. But certainly the construction of nuclear plants was a dangerous way to recover from identity confusion in Japan after the war

Looking back at the process, surprisingly, it was in the 1970s when *Space Battleship Yamato* and *Japan Sinking* were released and when nuclear plants began to spring up all over the country. Perhaps the social anxiety in the 1970s, although veiled by such events as the oil shock, was caused by the spread of nuclear plants: Japan embraced nuclear plants at a time when the threat of nuclear testing was still raw, and without having worked through the trauma of the A-bombs. Now, after 3/11, what was once denied in the past has come to the surface.

With regard to the safety of nuclear power, the former management of the Tokyo Electric Power Company (TEPCO) and former officials charged with nuclear power safety recalled: "We did recognize the insufficiency of our safety measures but no one would have dealt with them had someone raised concerns" (Independent Investigation Commission on the Fukushima Daiichi Nuclear Accident, 2012). Those on the operation side and those on the regulation side developed a cosy relationship, and, instead of working logically, they stressed an emotional oneness. People became more anxious and confused after they discovered that information had been withheld by the government and TEPCO, and realised that the effects of radiation exposure had been deliberately underestimated. As noted in Nakane's description of Japan's social structure, it is easy for a group to forego reason and even considerations of justice, at times leading to irrational and irresponsible decision making.

Despite this, those nuclear plants that were shut down after the disasters are about to resume operation due to so-called economic reasons. This is a clear example of a traumatised society repeating its injurious strategies. Trying to develop a society without taking care of its anxiety will increase latent anxieties and psychological dissociations at the social level. Ironically, Japan is in a state of massification for this very reason, with many of its people eagerly wanting strong leadership, especially in political and economic matters. They want the kind of leader who will allow them to deny their anxieties and enjoy a heroic solution in the real world. Thus, massification is activated to defend people against aggregation, and there is most likely an oscillation of elements of each.

Further discussion

Two processes occur in Japan following a major disaster. In the case of natural disasters, public reactions follow characteristic dynamics that have been engraved in Japan's foundation matrix. That is, because of strong survivor guilt, people work in silence, embracing grief, thus leading to social masochism. These dynamics do not confuse national identity. On the other hand, in the case of "man-made" disasters, such as wars and accidents, characteristic reactions are influenced by (and enhanced by) chosen traumas, with untreated traumas relapsing, thereby shaking national identity. These two processes are intertwined and unfold on a level that involves the whole of society. In other words, as a country, Japan is trying to seal her past trauma by marginalising damage from radiation, whereas the people of Fukushima are masochistically enduring their hardship. In addition, we must not forget the fact that they are under the threat of real radioactive substances at this very moment. Numbness from the fear of annihilation is also a traumatic reaction to a chronic stress.

Self-sacrificing commitment, labour, and isolation are virtues that are valued in Japan, a country where tragic heroes are admired. This applies to various groups in Japan today. Thirty thousand people commit suicide in Japan every year. Bullying at school sometimes leads victims to commit suicide, but, tragically, their suicides are hardly noticed. Apparently, harassment in sports clubs and overwork in companies are endless, sometimes leading to death. Such deaths stand in stark contrast to the mass shootings and murders that occur in schools and companies in the USA. In Japan, it is considered virtuous to keep working, enduring pain, and sacrificing the self rather than retreating from work, complaining to others, or resisting oppression. When economic crisis or trauma affects a group and organisation in Japanese society, individual members become isolated and form an aggregated group, often resulting in massification and leading individuals to self-ruin. The same dynamics may be seen at work both in the suicidal attack of Kamikaze pilots in wartime, and in the drive to achieve rapid economic growth after the war. Perhaps the processes seen in the affected areas are merely representations and personifications of these ways of Japanese society.

Conclusion

Clearly, it is difficult for a society that has experienced large-scale trauma. While oscillating between aggregation and massification to work through that trauma, the Japanese experience demonstrates that it is even more difficult to deal with new traumas subsequently occurring in endless years. Japan went so far as to accept "peaceful utilisation" of dreaded nuclear energy in order to deny its trauma and achieve economic and/or military growth. This is a dangerous heroic solution on a large scale that has been repeated in spite of recent failures.

The denial of trauma leads to several forms of expression. While the image of a heroic solution might bring people partial relief from latent threats, it can be abused by the same people who have become isolated in societies of aggregation. When hopes for the coming of a hero increase, people create massified cults led by pathological leaders. The same process can be seen in the political and economic world. Japan today is looking blindly for such a strong leader.

Before I end this chapter, I remind you of the Japanese foundation matrix. It has been seen that Japan has confronted several identity crises in the past, and each time sought rescue by trying to equate itself with so-called advanced countries. Japan's foundation matrix nurtures praise for tragic heroes: people sacrifice themselves to serve others and in order to overcome their sense of loss. Victims and non-victims share the same matrix. However, striving to stay strong while denying its own social trauma results in self-deception, continuing to confuse the identity of the nation with that of the individual. We need to further understand Japan's social unconscious. Without true dialogue, politically and interpersonally, providing space to authentically work through society's collective traumatic experience, this self-sacrificing pattern will not end.

Notes

1. It is a Japanese custom to cremate the dead body. After that, the relatives put pieces of the bone into a pot that is to be buried under a tombstone.
2. Nuttman-Shwartz & Weinberg (2012) analyse the *Sabra* in Israel from the viewpoint of the social unconscious. The *Sabra* is a heroic character who stands against all pressures, and one who has adopted enlightened and humanistic social values. This can be explained as a counter-reaction to the vulnerability of the Jews, who have a history of persecution. The authors go on to examine Israel as a society with trauma, from the perspective of the oscillation between massification and aggregation.

References

De Mendelssohn, F. (2008). Transgenerational transmission of trauma: guilt, shame, and the 'Heroic Dilemma'. *International Journal of Group Psychotherapy, 58*(3): 389–401.

Doi, T. (1973). *The Anatomy of Dependence: The Key Analysis of Japanese Behavior*. New York: Kodansha International.

Foulkes, S. H. (1973). The group as matrix of the individuals' mental life. In: E. Foulkes (Ed.), *S. H. Foulkes Selected Papers* (pp. 223–234). London: Karnac, 1990.

Freud, S. (1916a). On transience. *S. E., 14*: 303–307. London: Hogarth.

Gampel, Y., & Mazor, A. (2004). Intimacy and family links of adults who were children during the Shoah: multi-faceted mutations of the traumatic encapsulations. *Free Associations*, *11*: 546–568.

Hopper, E. (1981). *Social Mobility: A Study of Social Control and Insatiability*. Oxford: Blackwell.

Hopper, E. (2003a). *The Social Unconscious: Selected Papers*. London: Jessica Kingsley.

Hopper, E. (2003b). *Traumatic Experience in the Unconscious Life of Groups: The Fourth Basic Assumption: Incohesion: Aggregation/ Massification or (ba) I:A/M*. London: Jessica Kingsley.

Hopper, E. (Ed.) (2012). *Trauma and Organizations*. London: Karnac.

Hopper, E., & Weinberg, H. (2011). *The Social Unconscious in Persons, Groups, and Societies Volume 1: Mainly Theory*. London: Karnac.

Joyu, F. (2012). *Oumu Jiken 17-nenme no Kokuhaku* [AUM Incidents: Confession after 17 years]. Tokyo: Fusosha.

Murakami, H. (2001)[1997]. *Underground: The Tokyo GAS Attack and the Japanese Psyche*. London: Vintage Books.

Murakami, H. (2001)[1998].*Yakusokusareta Bashode-Anda-guraundo 2* [In the Place that Was Promised: Underground Two]. Tokyo: Bunshunbunko.

Murakami, H. (2011). As an unrealistic dreamer. [English translation of his acceptance speech on receiving the Catalunya International Prize 2011]. http://www.senrinomichi.com/?p=2728

Nakane, C. (1973). *Japanese Society* (revised edn). Harmondsworth, Penguin.

Nuttman-Shwartz, O., & Weinberg, H. (2012). Organizations in traumatized societies: the Israeli case. In: E. Hopper (Ed.), *Trauma and Organizations* (pp. 215–231). London: Karnac.

Pines, M. (2003). Foreword. In: Hopper (2003), *Traumatic Experience in the Unconscious Life of Groups: The Fourth Basic Assumption: Incohesion: Aggregation/Massification or (ba) I:A/M* (pp. 9–10). London: Jessica Kingsley.

Singer, T., & Kimbles, S. (Eds.) (2004). *The Cultural Complex: Contemporary Jungian Perspectives on Psyche and Society*. London: Brunner-Routledge.

Volkan, V. (2001). Transgenerational transmissions and chosen traumas: an aspect of large group identity. *Group Analysis*, *34*(1): 79–97.

Volkan, V. (2002). September 11th and societal regression. *Group Analysis*, *35*(4): 456–483.

Weinberg, H. (2007). So what is the social unconscious anyway? *Group Analysis*, *40*(3): 307–322.

Yoshii, H. (2008). *Gojira, Mosura, Gensuibaku: Tokusatsueiga no Shakaigaku* [Godzilla, Mothra, and the Atomic and Hydrogen Bombs]. Tokyo: Serikashobo.

CHAPTER SEVEN

The Irish social unconscious in relation to disability

Alan Corbett and Tamsin Cottis

Introduction

This chapter discusses some of the social, cultural, political, and economic aspects and elements of the foundation matrix of Ireland, and how these impact upon attitudes towards people with intellectual disabilities. Several comparisons are made with such aspects of the foundation matrix of England. We explore the idea that these matrices can be understood in terms of the social unconscious of the English and Irish peoples. A clinical vignette from a group analysis of patients with intellectual disabilities in Dublin is used to illustrate these hypotheses. The authors also draw on their personal and professional experiences in Ireland and in England. Alan Corbett's (AC) observations are coloured by his status as a "second generation" Irish man, occupying a liminal space between these two countries, and shaped by the interplay of generations, nationality, class, religion, sex, and gender norms. His interest in this topic stems from his work as a psychotherapist with patients with intellectual disabilities in Ireland and England, in the course of which he has noted the differences in the attitudes towards intellectual disability among the patients, members of their families, their carers, and their psychotherapists.

Tamsin Cottis (TC) has worked for twenty-five years with people with intellectual disabilities of all ages. Her work has been exclusively in England and Wales, first as teacher and then a psychotherapist.

Intellectual disability: its stigma and traumatic impact

Attitudes towards people with intellectual disabilities tend to be shaped to a significant degree by a complex interplay of fear, revulsion and denigration. Shah (1992) argues that the "stigma" of intellectual disability transcends race, beliefs, and culture, and is deeply embedded in terror, disgust, and hatred, as well as in rejecting and punitive attitudes towards people who have intellectual disabilities (Corbett, 2011). Their quality of life tends to be low, involving experiences, for example, of social marginalisation, poverty, poor health outcomes, and unemployment (Petry et al., 2005).

There is a high prevalence of trauma in the lives of people with disabilities, both at birth for the baby and mother, and at subsequent phases of development (Cottis, 2009). A developmental view of attachment shows how the securely attached, well-loved child does better at school, through the latency period, and beyond. Poor relational experiences in infancy are shown to have an impact on later capacity to form positive relationships. The child with intellectual disabilities might find it difficult to make friends and to achieve status through school-based achievement. Thus, the pervasive influence of the social unconscious in the first stages of life can become a self-fulfilling prophecy as the disabled child falls progressively further behind social norms and expectations in terms of their personal and professional experience. The ego strength and sense of self of the growing child and adolescent might be weakened. People with disabilities are four times more likely than those without disabilities to experience various forms of abuse (Sobsey, 1994). People with intellectual disabilities are disproportionately vulnerable to sexual exploitation (Brown et al., 1995; McCormack et al., 2005).

Clinical resistance to treating people with intellectual disabilities (Bender, 1993) combined with the view that they are inherently inferior because they have limited earning power (Marks, 1999) has resulted in their rarely receiving appropriate treatment at the appropriate time, and in being denied the help that they need in order to address their experiences of abuse and trauma. "Society" acts out its hatred and disdain of people with disabilities by denying them the services they need. This can be seen most concretely in the failure adequately to fund necessary support, such as early intervention initiatives, therapy to help with emotional problems, and funding to help those organisations which seek to provide psychological support to people with disabilities and their families (McGinnity & Banks, 2004).

Most Western societies tend to privilege a baby's intelligence more highly than its gender. To deal with the birth of a baby with an intellectual disability requires a combination of emotional maturity, resilience, and, crucially, societal support. What is called for, but rarely achieved, is a mother's capacity to mourn the loss of the longed for "perfect" child and the society's ability to contain that mourning. Both societal and maternal matrices of responses are similar: shock, guilt, shame, fear, hatred, and difficulties in authentically mourning the loss that has occurred. Blackman (2003) describes how lack of opportunities to grieve can lead to insecure attachment experiences, and complicated grief responses to subsequent losses.

The social context: England and Wales

In England and Wales, children and young people with diagnosed special education needs have a statutory right to education until age twenty-three. For adults, the situation is far worse. Services are sparse and are persistently under attack through lack of funding, especially since 2010. The prospect of the lifelong dependence of the adult, and the concomitant absence of hope—summarised as "the situation is never going to get better and this person is always going to need more support than others"—is hard for a capitalist economy to bear, especially when under stress. The recent coalition government targeted the least economically productive citizens in their efforts to reduce national spending on welfare. It is estimated that people with the most severe disabilities face cuts nineteen times greater than those faced by a typical member of the community who is not disabled (Butler et al., 2013). The daily experience of bullying, abuse, and discrimination faced by people with intellectual disabilities shows that there is still a long way to go before top-down legislative and social reform affects the social unconscious. Furthermore, political theorists such as

Gilligan (2011) and Wilkinson and Pickett (2010) argue that the more economically polarised a nation becomes, the greater the instance of violence and abuse perpetrated towards those perceived as vulnerable or different.

From the late 1970s, there have been radical developments in the politics of disability. Alongside arguments for "normalisation", the American sociologist Wolfensberger and others identified the right of people with intellectual disabilities to speak up for themselves and to experience in society "social role valorisation" (Wolfensberger, 1992). Such ideas underpinned the development of the self advocacy movement. This thinking found a foothold in North America and in Scandinavia and also in England. The idea that emphasis in care for people with intellectual disabilities should be on common humanity, rather than difference, has become highly influential in social policy and service provision. Perhaps the most marked expression of this came in the Government White Paper of 2001, "Valuing People", with its clearly stated message that, in terms of provision for people with intellectual disabilities and their families, there should be *"Nothing About Us without Us"*. While many of the ideals and aims of the White Paper have not been fulfilled, largely due to a failing commitment to extra financial resources, its essential values base has not been challenged. Those values challenge the very idea of the "specialness" of special needs. Rather, the changes to services that people with intellectual disabilities require are seen through the lens of equalities legislation; that is, services should be available equally to all people. Services might need to adapt to make this possible, but the onus is on them to do so and if they fail in this, they will be in contravention of the law. This can perhaps be seen most strikingly in the provision of education where, increasingly, children with identified special educational needs are educated in mainstream schools, alongside their non-disabled peers. There have also been a number of recent challenges to government decisions—some successful—based on the argument that the proposed cut has a disproportionate affect on people with disabilities. Clearly, such a statement of values partly reflects and partly creates a complex set of social attitudes towards people with disabilities, and it is possible to see how, notwithstanding the current acute economic pressures, this could lead to change in the social attitudes towards people with intellectual disabilities. Arguably, the legislative picture in Ireland does not facilitate a change in the same way.

The social context: Ireland

The social unconscious of the people of any country is constrained and restrained by the history and structure of its society. Ireland has a complex history of conflict, famine, colonial subjugation, economic volatility, religious oppression, and clerical abuse (Foster, 2001; Garvin, 2004; Toibin & Ferriter, 2001). Edna O'Brien, in her auto-biography, Mother Ireland (1976), writes,

> Countries are either fathers or mothers, and engender the emotional bristle secretly reserved for either sire. Ireland has always been a woman, a womb, a cave, a cow, a Rosaleen, a sow, a bride, a harlot, and, of course, the gaunt Hag of Beare. Originally a land of woods and thickets, such as Orpheus had seen when prescribing the voyage of Jason, through a misted atmosphere. She is thought to have known invasion from the time when the ice age ended and the improving climate allowed deer to throng her dense forest. These infiltrations have been told and fabricated by men and by mediums who described the violation of her soul. Ireland has always been god ridden. (p. 12)

Ireland's God is a Catholic God. The interdependence of church and state in the development of a national identity (Garvin, 2004) ensured for centuries that people's sexuality was repressed, and the role of women was traditionally one of servitude to the family. It is likely that over the past twenty years this situation has changed with the impact of feminism, the dissolution of church control, the Europeanisation of Irish society and revelations of widespread clerical abuse of children and young people. The reporting of these revelations (Ryan, 2009) was interpreted by many as the final nail in the coffin of Catholic control over the Irish nation, cataloguing, as it did, decades of widespread and systemic sexual and physical abuse of children and adults in the care of the church, many of whom had intellectual dis-abilities. The close detailing of abuse perpetrated by those at the apex of Irish society unleashed an unprecedented level of revulsion and outrage that may be viewed as the middle stage of a process of trans-formation that has been preceded by legislative changes such as the introduction of divorce and the decriminalisation of homosexuality.

Ireland's complex colonial relationship with Britain, its struggle for independence, its enmeshed relationship with Catholicism, its history of neutrality in international warfare, its place as an island and its legacy of famine, displacement, and the diaspora, have all been recon-figured over the past decade. Historically, when times were hard, Ireland lost its young. The birth of the Celtic Tiger reversed this situation. Ireland not only kept its citizens, but also attracted those of other countries. However, the death of the Celtic Tiger has led Ireland to revert to its position of exporting its young. Naturally, this has also led to a reconfiguration of many attitudes to social life and sexuality in particular.

Irish social unconscious in relation to intellectual disability

Both Irish and English peoples struggle to process unconscious fear and hatred of people with intellectual disabilities. Whereas it can be argued that Irish attitudes tend to be rooted in social shame, English attitudes tend to be more rooted in England's industrial and economic history. The care and treatment of people with intellectual disabilities in England has been influenced by the fear the "feeble-minded" would contaminate wider society. In contemporary England, there is wide-spread ante-natal screening of increasing technical sophistication. If a mother chooses to continue with a pregnancy in the knowledge that her baby will be born with a disability she might be viewed as foolish, or irresponsible. The baby might be viewed as a potential drain on societal as well as family resources. In Ireland, however, where abortion on the grounds of disability is not allowed, it would be regarded as sinful to terminate the pregnancy. From a political perspective, the tide of "normalisation" (Flynn & Lemay, 1999; French, 1994; Oliver, 1998) towards disabilities in England in the 1980s did not occur in Ireland. Normalisation in Britain drew on social models of disability (Marks, 1999) that viewed social interventions as being as, or more, disabling of people's potential than their primary disability. Influenced by social constructionist theory (Clegg, 1993) and running concur-rently with a Care in the Community political strategy that moved substantial numbers of people with intellectual disabilities from large, long-stay institutions into smaller group home settings (Mansell et al., 2002), normalisation influenced those being trained in social care to adopt a less paternalistic view of their clients, to adapt their interven-tions and the tools to empower the individual, and to view those with intellectual disabilities as people first, regardless of their disabilities.

Sexuality and sex education

O'Driscoll (2009) points to the historical fears—once overtly expressed, now carried more unconsciously, though still powerfully (Hollins & Grimer, 1988)—that there is something inherently dangerous in the sexuality of people with intellectual disabilities, whether this be through uncontrolled reproduction, illegitimacy, or their supposedly rampant sexual desires. Significant shifts in government policy regarding people with intellectual disabilities have also had an impact upon patterns of sexuality. In contrasting the life of persons with an intellectual disability in England in, say, 2013, to their life in 1983, we can see that in 2013 they had greater access to sex education, delivered in a manner appropriate to their level of understanding, and underpinned by an acknowledgement of each of them as a sexual being. The lack of an Irish policy of normalisation in the 1980s has caused people with intellectual disabilities in 2013 to lag behind their UK equivalents. We are not idealising the current situation: the sexual lives of people with intellectual disabilities in the UK in 2013 continued to be subject to many more violations of privacy and respect than their non-disabled peers. However, many of the changes have been enshrined in law. Care was taken in the formulation of Section 4 of the reform of Sexual Offences Act (2003) to try to balance the sexual rights of those with intellectual disabilities with their need for extra protection in some circumstances.

Clinical responses to disability

It is important to distinguish emotional intelligence from cognitive intelligence (Galton, 2002). In providing psychotherapy for people with intellectual disabilities, it is necessary for the therapist to make changes to his/her vocabulary: for example, avoiding polysyllabic and multi-meaning interventions. The pace of intervention can be adapted, in order to accommodate the patient's slower rate of cognitive processing. Also, avoiding an overly "neutral" and unresponsive attitude that might exacerbate the patient's feelings of shame, guilt, or terror in thinking about her emotions is especially helpful. Sinason's development of the concept of secondary handicap, as well as her work on the impact of early abuse on disability, her recognition of the phenomenon of somatised trauma as presented by patients with intellectual disabilities, and her work with sex offenders with intellectual disabilities have all been exceedingly helpful to practitioners in this specialised field.

The responses of the mother to her disabled baby overlap those of "society" to her disabled baby. Sobsey's "ecological model" illustrates how the core attachments, so essential to the development of a strong sense of self, are under attack because of society's message, carried in the social unconscious, that this child is not worth developing a relationship with. However, Alvarez (1992) has described the role of the therapist as an enlivener, literally bringing to life a mind that is damaged by trauma, autism, or disability. The therapist as enlivener may also be an unconscious response to society's death wish towards those with disabilities. The experience of having a child who is damaged, or undesired, and whose birth, because of feelings about disability which reside in the social unconscious, cannot be celebrated, has a critical impact on early relational development. Alvarez's work demonstrates that children with disabilities can experience, through psychoanalytic psychotherapy, a growing capacity to make sense of themselves, and of themselves in relation to others. They can come to experience themselves as enjoyable and enjoyed. Unlike therapy with a person who has experienced trauma or damage from which they need to recover or be repaired, Alvarez sees her work as often to be in the very construction of the self.

Hopper (2012) has written of the very particular challenges faced by individuals and organisations who are engaged in providing psychotherapy to people with intellectual disabilities.

Clinical vignette

In order to examine the Irish social unconscious in relation to disability, we have used data from group analysis conducted with patients with intellectual disabilities in Ireland. The group was a forensic one, using a matrix developed initially within a UK clinic (Corbett, 2013) in which the analytic group was conducted within a systemic intervention programme comprising four strands.

1. The analytic group, conducted by AC and a female colleague, with six male members. All had intellectual disabilities and forensic histories.

2. The carers group, conducted by two professionals. This took place at the same time as the analytic group, and was open to two members of the patients' support network, be they family member or member of staff. The group had, on average, eight members each week. These were mainly paid members of staff, though a small number of parents also attended. It had a structured psycho-educative syllabus, looking at issues such as risk management, sexuality, and disability, and the purpose and function of psychotherapy.

3. Quarterly training seminars for organisations, in which members of the team presented on issues such as relationships and sexuality in the lives of people with intellectual disabilities.

4. The project was researched, with a psychologist analysing pre- and post- group interviews with group members and their carers. The therapists also filled in questionnaires designed to assess changes in men's self esteem, ability to communicate with others, and development of insight.

The reasons for multiple interventions around the group therapy were rooted in:

(i)   the particular life experiences of people with intellectual disabilities;

(ii) the forensic histories of the group members.

The combination of (i) and (ii) requires an adaptation of the classical group analytic model (that is, a group on its own to which patients come on a regular basis, in the absence of any parallel interventions). The reasons for this are several. First, most of the group members lived in institutions, which were run by the church. Also, their level of disability and attendant deficits in social functioning meant that they depended on others both for referrals to the group and for staff who would accompany the patients to it. At an early stage of the group's development, it was additionally recognised that many of those caring for the men would struggle to understand and support the purpose and process of the analytic group, including some of the changes that they expected that the group could bring about in levels of assertion, self-esteem, and insight. There was a risk that this ambivalence would cause the carers unconsciously to sabotage the attendance. In anticipation of this, we provided a space in which their ambivalence and envy could be worked with, albeit under the guise of a psycho-educative support programme.

When compared with a similar group programme conducted in London (Corbett, 2013), a higher level of anxiety was demonstrated in the Irish settings. The lives of the men in the Irish group were highly regulated, with scant attention being paid to their human rights. One group member, for example, lived in a controlled setting in which a "shut down" policy had been implemented in response to the perceived level of sexual risk. He was accompanied by three members of staff, all of whom had been instructed never to engage him in any discussions relating to sexuality, and if he raised any such issues himself, they were compelled to "shut down" the conversation immediately. Other men were subject to similarly high levels of supervision and monitoring, despite the fact that some of them had not perpetrated any acts of sexual abuse for over twenty years.

The forensic history of the men was shrouded in anxiety and confusion. In assessing them for the group, there emerged a history of sexual experimentation that had been met in an overly punitive way. Kafkaesque narratives emerged. For example, an adolescent's staring at a woman's breasts had been reported as a sexual offence. Sexual experimentation between two adolescent men had been pathologised as a perverse attack. While English attitudes towards the sexuality of people with intellectual disabilities are hardly without fear, revulsion and anger, the severity of the responses to the Irish men indicated a

Catholic conflation of sex and sin, underscored by a deep abhorrence of expressions of homosexuality.

This is indicative of an Irish social unconscious that, in relation to disability, struggles with a "double-bind": sex that cannot result in procreation is regarded as inherently evil, but disabled people creating more disabled people is regarded as equally abhorrent. The person with a disability cannot then have sex that is not, in one way or another, regarded as sinful. The parallel group for carers became an important repository for many of the anxieties felt by those struggling both with painful emotional responses to the men for whom they were paid to care and the system in which they worked—a system many were eventually able to question and challenge. Without this group, I doubt whether the analytic group for the men would have survived, vulnerable as it tended to be to systemic sabotage (Hopper, 2012).

The clinical material that follows is from the first few months of a new group for men with intellectual disabilities. AC's colleague was absent from this session. The material has been anonymised.

> The group began with the men paying their weekly fee (a minimal contribution to the running of the group), alongside much manic laughter and derogatory comments directed at each other. I let the group know that my co-conductor was not here today. The men nodded, and did not ask any questions. I wondered aloud if the group recalled where we got to last session. Someone remembered we had talked about God. Someone said he was thinking about me during the week, wondering about whether I had children. Others voiced their questions: what football team I supported, where I live, what part of England I came from, and so on. After my interpreting the frustrations about me withholding from them, someone began to sing an anti-English song. After this, two group members disclosed memories of death and loss. Someone asked if I would put away the money that was on the table. I linked this to the group's thoughts about temptation, and wondering that, if things are laid out on the table, would the group be more likely to succumb to temptation?

> Someone voiced his worries that I would think about my own children when they talked about paedophilia. I thought they might be working out whether they could trust me to hear about what was in their heads. I said that the group was working out how much they could bring their real selves into the group space. Would I reject them, or hate them, or fear them? Or would I accept them and offer them something nurturing?

> We spent some time looking at the different ways in which the men were relating to the group, how some were highly engaged, and some less so.

This elicited from one, previously quiet, man descriptions of the abuses that had referred him to the group. His description left me confused, although the group seemed to understand fully the bizarre and contradictory descriptions he gave, and voiced unusually strong declarations of support for him, and a desire for him to never leave the group.

A highly personal statement about suicide followed, prompting a very visual response of shock, revulsion, and fear from the group. Another man began to talk (in a jocular manner) about how he had acquired his brain injury, prompting others' recollections. Someone said he felt all right about talking about paedophilia. This was not taken up. Instead, there was a return to discussion about brains, and how they get injured. A more able group member described his strategies for managing sexual thoughts. Many descriptions of journeys encumbered by intrusive sadistic sexual fantasies ensued.

We ended by returning to lots of questions being put to me—am I married, what car I drive, where I live, etc. There was a further discussion about how much I can be trusted, with a detailed analysis of how I sit in my chair, and how this proves I am married, have children, and drive a certain kind of car. They took some time to leave. Someone joked to another man, "You are the weakest link—goodbye!" Another said, "We're all the weakest links till next week."

The indignity of no labour

The group began by touching on two central strands of the social unconscious of Irish people in relation to disability—poverty and unemployment. The handing over of the men's money might appear at first sight to be a fairly normal part of the fabric of a mainstream group's life, enacted as it was with a swaggering potency, a broadbrush painting of "men at work", handing over the toils of their labour. Yet, for all these men, there is no dignity of labour, for there is no labour. They spent most of their time in day centres, sometimes taking part in fairly mindless activities with others, but more often doing nothing. When asked more about what they did, one man had described "*looking* at the papers", in a heartbreakingly precise way. He could not read or write, so looking rather than reading was all he could do. In this way, the minds of the men remained dead, because nothing enlivening was allowed to happen to them. This can be thought of as a murderous attack upon the disabled, the responsive enactment of a societal death wish. Something annihilatory is being enacted through which the men have been placed in settings devoid of stimulation or thought, where their minds atrophy from disuse.

Without a political and economic will to maintain the social and legal progress which has been made in England since the advent of normalisation, the power of the social unconscious (including the hatred and frustration that life-long dependence can engender) might help to prop up the view that some disadvantaged members of our society are "undeserving" of societal support. Building on Sinason's (1986) notion of a secondary handicap being a defence against trauma that is separate from the primary, congenital, organic disability, this might be described as a "tertiary handicap"; a societal disablement, informed by the need for the mess and pain of disability to be kept firmly in its non-thinking location. The social starvation of the minds of such men is another responsive enactment of the societal wish to murder them.

The poverty of disability

This death wish is glimpsed, too, in the men's relationship with money. Their income was restricted (and shortly to be restricted yet further as Ireland's economic meltdown results in disability benefit being cut to the bone) and the money they handed me had, in its turn, been handed to them by members of staff who controlled their income and expenditure in a way that echoed global events unfolding around the group. At the time of this group, Ireland was still struggling to process its national shame at being the recipient of "bail-out" money from the rest of the EU—something experienced as both a deep narcissistic wound and a societal castration. The Irish social unconscious in relation to disability had contributed to a castration of these men, representing, as they did, a challenge to notions of normality, potency, and capacity for procreation. Not unlike men I have treated in a forensic group in England, they lived on the bottom rung of society's ladder, but for these men in this particular society, that rung was also suffused with Ireland's paradigm of Catholic shame, famine, and poverty. There existed, too, an echo of Ireland's relationship with colonial Britain, in the men handing over the fruits of their "labour" to the English landowner. This reflected a powerful, underpinning dynamic that is rarely far from the surface when English and Irish interrelate: the echo of the famine and the stripping away of Irish life and dignity by the English in "the shambles of our history" (Maloy, 1998). The singing of the anti-English song could be heard as a howl of rage stemming from the collective unconscious of bereaved and traumatised Ireland having to pay its dues for torture yet again.

The role of God

The place of God in the group's material points to a transferential process in which my role as group conductor was coloured and shaped by the group's lived experiences as men disabled by both their cognitive deficits and by the society in which they had developed. I was experienced as the terrifying, sadistic, "death-making" (Wolfensberger, 1987) God who had caused their brains not to work and their lives to be underpinned by poverty, trauma, parental ambivalence, loss, and extreme marginalisation; a harsh superego figure who had created these men not only as disabled beings, but also as men who have been abused and who (might) have gone on to abuse others. Their questions about my personal life can be thought about as their way of researching whether I will be the judgemental God-like being who looks on them, their disabilities, and their abusive actions with disgust and hate, or whether I will be someone able to see their abusive actions as a defence against unbearable loss and pain. Their intense need to deconstruct me, to perform a vivisection in the operating theatre of the group room, spoke of their desperate awareness of cognitive failure, parental ambivalence, and societal hatred. They yearned for an omniscient or omnipotent God who would magically remove the trauma embodied within both their disability and their sexual desires.

Sexual aggression and the social unconscious

While the aetiology of sexual aggression is, of course, complex and multi-layered, the disproportionately high levels of sexual dysfunction and perversion in the intellectually disabled population (presenting as both victims and perpetrators) (Corbett, 1996; Craig & Hutchinson,

2005; Holland et al., 2002; Lindsay & Taylor, 2005) must be understood in the context of the foundation matrix. A question that resonated through the life of this group was that of why they had done what they had done, or why the world had responded to what they had not quite done. As the group progressed, its members became more alive and more interested in the questions of both their forensic history and why they had been born, or made, disabled. It is no coincidence that this group's discussion of how someone's brain had been injured was quickly followed by someone else wanting to talk about paedophilia, a wish denied and responded to with a re-examination of how the group's minds had been disabled. The sexual abuse of people with intellectual disabilities in Ireland remains largely shrouded in denial. In comparison with a similar group of patients treated in an English setting (Corbett, 2013), disclosures of childhood abuse by this group of Irish men tended to be minimised, denied, or ignored, indicating a particularly Irish and Catholic aversion to the notion of sexual experiences being part of the life story of a person with a intellectual disability. This denial extended to the men's later expressions of sexual need. Some of the acts of sexual offending attributed to the men could be interpreted as expressions of sexual frustration rather than pathological intent. The Irish social unconscious in relation to disability is partly informed by a powerful need to disavow sexual desire within the disabled, resulting in an exaggerated tendency to interpret normal sexual desires as sinful, abnormal, and abusive.

The social unconscious in relation to disability, as expressed by carers

The parallel group run for the carers of the men was designed primarily as a psycho-educative experience for members of staff (and some family members). They held much of the responsibility for monitoring and managing the men's supposedly sexually aggressive behaviours. The creative partnership of the group's conductors—an educationalist and a psychotherapist—allowed the group to talk (in most cases for the first time) about their ambivalence towards the men they were presumed to care for and, in some cases, love. The death of the Celtic Tiger during the lifetime of this group enabled hatred of disability to be conceptualised in a strongly expressed wish to annihilate these troublesome men who cost so much to house and manage, and who were seen to be starving other (more deserving, less dangerous) men and women with intellectual disabilities of scarce and shrinking resources. Discussions about these feelings were initially tentative, contradicting as they did the overarching desire to be seen as a good group of good people, dutifully caring for the disabled in ways that reflected the ethos of the church-run organisations that employed them.

The fact of my English accent (and my imagined Englishness) enabled some examination of their ambivalence towards the British colonial coming over to guard, imprison, or punish these troublesome forensic subjects. I was imagined to have come from the former colonial power that had fought in a war in which the Irish were neutral (in this case, a forensic war in which England was presumed to have fought for knowledge of how to treat forensic patients with disabilities), knowledge felt to have been scant or missing within Ireland itself. Thus, I oscillated between being perceived as personifying both the Irish social unconscious and the English social unconscious. On the one hand, the omnipotent Irish God struggling with the ambivalence of caring for those whose lives could not be aborted, and, on the other, the object able to view these men as deserving of psychological and real homes in which their human rights could be respected, and where their abilities as much as their disabilities could be held equally in mind. To be a therapist with patients with intellectual disabilities requires an analysis of the countertransference that is somewhat more than the usual struggle to consider the impact of our own individual relationship with disability. It also requires a capacity to observe how we are inevitably coloured and shaped though the influence of a foundation matrix that discriminates so powerfully against those with disabilities.

Systemic issues

To work with those with cognitive deficits and histories of gross sexual trauma, an analytic group on its own, in isolation, is not enough. An analytic group, particularly a forensic group, must be supported in a system of parallel groups for core staff and administrators. Twenty-plus years experience in a London-based psychotherapy clinic for people with intellectual disabilities has led to the development of an integrative clinical model that is informed by psychotherapeutic thinking as well as an understanding of the influence of a social unconscious. The Respond Clinical Model, described by Blackman and Cottis (2014), places parallel work with the client network at the heart of the psychotherapeutic process. The aim of this parallel work is to effect relational change between client and carers. It provides a developmentally informed framework, which encompasses an understanding of the power of the social unconscious, to enhance the quality of the emotional support and treatment and resources available to patients with intellectual disabilities.

The disability within, and the role of sin

The impoverished status of Ireland across the centuries has become "located" within its intellectually disabled population, whose sense of powerlessness is continually reinforced through its banishment to the margins of society where paid work is an empty fantasy and life is lived on the thinnest of incomes. While the Irish social unconscious is inevitably coloured by intense feelings of shame about being colonised, either by another state or a church that subsumed the state (Garvin, 2004), notions of sex and sexuality mired in sin and poverty are rarely far from the surface. In relation to disability, these dynamics are enacted most vividly, expressing a tendency to stigmatise, exclude, and pathologise. Within the Irish social unconscious, attitudes towards the living and the dying of the disabled tend to be even more complex and contradictory than those within the English social unconscious, partially underpinned as they are by Catholic Ireland's view of abortion as a mortal sin being enshrined in restrictive legislation. English procedures for antenatal screening, and the availability of termination in the event of diagnosed disability, can be experienced as a communication of the view that "it would be better if such lives did not occur". While not understating the individual agonies which are experienced by families who face such a choice, the situation is perhaps still more complicated in Ireland, where abortion cannot be considered if the only reason for it is that the foetus is disabled. In Ireland, the life is apparently no less valuable than the non-disabled life. But what is to happen to feelings of hate, sadness, anger, and grief, where no choice to avoid the disabled life was offered? The social unconscious becomes further complicated.

Attitude towards sin is the key factor that differentiates the social unconscious in relation to disability in Ireland from that in England. For example, in Ireland, for a mother to abort (or even consider aborting) her disabled foetus is regarded as a sin, a perverse negation of maternal drives. In England, a mother who decides to keep her disabled baby is subject to the disapproval of society. The mother in England with her disabled baby tends to be regarded as having contravened the unwritten rules of society. The baby is a drain, sucking society dry and disturbing its notions of acceptable normality. However, the Irish disabled baby is a test from God, the cross that has to be borne, the penance that is ultimately seen as redemptive. The baby embodies sin just as much as sex without marriage does. People with intellectual disabilities do not get married in Ireland, and, thus, their sexual desires must remain as expression of sinfulness—perversion that must be disavowed. In both societies, people with intellectual disabilities are receptacles of projective hatred, but for fundamentally different reasons. The English mother pushing her pram is scorned because her baby should never have been born. The Irish mother pushing her pram is a saint. It is her baby that carries the sin.

Conclusion

Ireland's history of trauma, as both an invaded and colonised land and a starved country, helps constitute its foundation matrix and informs its relationship with disability. In considering Ireland's status as a colonised land, we are thinking not just of 900 years of English rule, but also of its colonisation by the Catholic Church, and the myriad ways in which church and state have interrelated and merged (Garvin, 2004). We have chosen intellectual disability as a lens through which to view the foundation matrices of England and Ireland because it personifies many aspects of the matrix. To have an intellectual disability in Ireland is to be subject to punishment for sins of the body and of the mind. Punishment is afforded through the systemic impoverishment of those with disabilities, the consigning of the disabled to church-run settings in which their sexual needs and desires will be feared and ignored, and the paranoid supervision and monitoring of sexual desire. Disability has the power to disturb individual and social defences and to magnify aspects of the social unconscious rooted in shame, fear, and disdain.

Disability stirs up primitive defences that are as much to do with disability as they are to do with sexuality, gender, and the body. What is projected into those with disabilities serves to illustrate a particular defensive position in relation to disability. It also underscores our own individual and social struggles to accommodate our own sense of disability, usually by disavowing them in ourselves and then evacuating them into the disabled other. Desire and disability are regarded as antithetical, the conflation of both being a challenge to societal notions of the disabled as being neutered, sexless creatures for whom desire can only be thought of as a form of sadistic attack.

The relationship between England and Ireland is a complex one, but also one that contains many similarities with other neighbouring territories. Most societies seem to need a neighbour they can denigrate and disparage. Just as Ireland can hate England for its colonial history, the English can disparage the Irish for their "stupidity": the image of the "thick Paddy" is a stereotype that is difficult to give up. Stripped of much of their past colonial potency, it seems that England still needs to feel some power by relating to Ireland as a handicapped, and intellectually impoverished, fool. The attribution of intelligence continues to be a powerful medium for superiority and denigration.

We have focused here mainly on features of the social unconscious with respect to disability in Ireland and in England. We have presented clinical material that illustrates the complex and highly punitive attitudes and behaviour of the members of the group towards their disabilities. This is something akin to internalised homophobia or internalised racism—an introjection of society's disavowal of the different. We hope to study these processes in more detail in our future work.

References

Alvarez, A. (1992). *Live Company: Psychoanalytic Psychotherapy with Autistic, Borderline, Deprived and Abused Children*. London: Routledge.

Bender, M. (1993). The unoffered chair: the history of therapeutic disdain towards people with a learning difficulty. *Clinical Psychology Forum, 54*: 7–12.

Blackman, N. (2003). *Loss and Learning Disability*. London: Worth.

Blackman, N., & Cottis, T. (2014). *The Respond Clinical Model*. In press, Respond.

Brown, H., Stein, J., & Turk, V. (1995). The sexual abuse of adults with learning disabilities: report of a second two year incidence survey. *Mental Handicap Research, 8*(1): 22–24.

Butler, P., Taylor, M., & Ball, J. (2013). Welfare cuts will cost disabled people £28bn over five years. *The Guardian*, 23 March. Retrieved from http://www.theguardian.com/society/2013/mar/27/welfare-cuts-disabled-people

Clegg, J. A. (1993). Putting people first: a social constructionist approach to learning disability. *British Journal of Clinical Psychology, 32*(4): 389–406.

Corbett, A. (1996). *Trinity of Pain*. London: Respond.

Corbett, A. (2011). Silk purses and sows' ears: the social and clinical exclusion of people with intellectual disabilities. *Psychodynamic Practice, 17*(3): 273–290.

Corbett, A. (2013). The invisible men: forensic group therapy with people with intellectual disabilities. In: J. Woods & A. Williams (Eds.), *Forensic Group Psychotherapy: The Portman Approach* (pp. 183–201). London: Karnac.

Cottis, T. (2009). Love hurts: the emotional impact of intellectual disability and sexual abuse on a family. In: T. Cottis (Ed.), *Intellectual Disability, Trauma and Psychotherapy* (pp. 75–89). London: Routledge.

Craig, L. A., & Hutchinson, R. B. (2005). Sexual offenders with learning disabilities: risk, recidivism and treatment. *Journal of Sexual Aggression, 11*(3): 289–304.

Flynn, R. J., & Lemay, R. A. (1999). *A Quarter-century of Normalization and Social Role Valorization: Evolution and Impact*. Ottawa: University of Ottawa Press.

Foster, R. F. (2001). *Oxford Atlas of Irish History*. Oxford: Oxford University Press.

French, S. (1994). *On Equal Terms: Working with Disabled People*. Oxford: Butterworth/Heinemann.

Galton, G. (2002). New horizons in disability psychotherapy: the contributions of Valerie Sinason. *Free Associations, 9*: 582–610.

Garvin, T. (2004). *Preventing the Future: Why Was Ireland So Poor for So Long?* Dublin: Gill & MacMillan.

Gilligan, J. (2011). *Why Some Politicians Are More Dangerous than Others*. New York: Polity Press.

Holland, T., Clare, I. C. H., & Mukhopadhyay, T. (2002). Prevalence of 'criminal offending' by men and women with intellectual disability and the characteristics of 'offenders': implications for research and service development. *Journal of Intellectual Disability Research, 46*(s1): 6–20.

Hollins, S., & Grimer, M. (1988). *Going Somewhere: People with Mental Handicaps and their Pastoral Care.* London: SPCK.

Home Office (2003). *Sexual Offences Act.* London: Stationery Office.

Hopper, E. (2012). Some challenges to the capacity to think, link and hope in the provision of psychotherapy for the learning disabled. In: J. Adlam, A. Aiyegbusi, P. Kleinot, A. Motz, & C. Scanlon (Eds.), *The Therapeutic Milieu Under Fire: Security and Insecurity in Forensic Mental Health* (pp. 229–239). London: Jessica Kingsley.

Lindsay, W. R., & Taylor, J. L. (2005). A selective review of research on offenders with developmental disabilities: assessment and treatment. *Clinical Psychology & Psychotherapy, 12*(3): 201–214.

Maloy, K. E. (1998). Out of the shambles of our history: Irish women and (post)colonial identity. PhD dissertation. West Virginia University.

Mansell, J., Ashman, B., Macdonald, S., & Beadle-Brown, J. (2002). Residential care in the community for adults with intellectual disability: needs, characteristics and services. *Journal of Intellectual Disability Research, 46*(8): 8.

Marks, D. (1999). *Disability: Controversial Debates and Psychosocial Perspectives.* London: Routledge.

McCormack, B., Kavanagh, D., Caffrey, S., & Power, A. (2005). Investigating sexual abuse: findings of a 15-year longitudinal study. *Journal of Applied Research in Intellectual Disabilities, 18*(3): 217–227.

McGinnity, M., & Banks, R. (2004). *Psychotherapy and Learning Disability.* London: Royal College of Psychiatrists.

O'Brien, E. (1976). *Mother Ireland.* London: Weidenfeld & Nicholson.

O'Driscoll, D. (2009). Psychotherapy and intellectual disability. A historical view. In: T. Cottis (Ed.), *Intellectual Disability, Trauma and Psychotherapy* (pp. 9–28). London: Routledge.

Oliver, M. (1998). Theories in health care and research: theories of disability in health practice and research. *British Medical Journal, 317*(7170): 1446–1449.

Petry, K., Maes, B., & Vlaskamp, C. (2005). Domains of quality of life of people with profound multiple disabilities: the perspective of parents and direct support staff. *Journal of Applied Research in Intellectual Disabilities, 18*(1): 35–46.

Ryan, S. (2009). *Commission to Inquire into Child Abuse.* Dublin: Irish Government.

Shah, R. (1992). *The Silent Minority: Children with Disabilities in Asian Families.* London: National Children's Bureau.

Sinason, V. (1986). Secondary mental handicap and its relationship to trauma. *Psychoanalytic Psychotherapy,* 2(2): 131–154.

Sobsey, D. (1994). *Violence and Abuse in the Lives of People With Disabilities: The End of Silent Acceptance?* Baltimore, MD: Paul H Brookes.

Toibin, C., & Ferriter, D. (2001). *The Irish Famine.* London: Profile Books.

Wilkinson, R., & Pickett, K. (2010). *The Spirit Level: Why Equality Is Better for Everyone.* London: Penguin.

Wolfensberger, W. (1987). *The New Genocide of Handicapped and Afflicted People.* New York: Syracuse University Press.

Wolfensberger, W. (1992). *A Brief Introduction to Social Role Valorization.* New York: Syracuse University Press.

CHAPTER EIGHT

Reflections upon Brazilian social unconscious

Carla Penna

I n this contribution, I will explore various aspects of the Brazilian foundation matrix by means of an investigation into its historical roots, followed by reflections upon the "the existence and constraints of social, cultural and communicational arrangements of which [*Brazilian*] people are unaware" (Hopper & Weinberg, 2011, p. xxx). Brazil is a young country of huge dimensions; consequently, due to cultural, social, and economic diversities found in each of its regions, there is not just one Brazil, but many nations within a nation. The challenge of conceptualising the social unconscious of people from a country with a population of 201 million inhabitants (in 2014) is rather stimulating. However, based on the perspective of Foucault (1979) concerning the "apparatus of power" and the considerations of Dalal on the social unconscious as "the representation of the institutionalization of social power relations in the structure of the psyche itself" (Dalal, 1998, p. 210), this investigation will focus on the co-construction of power structures in the Brazilian foundation matrix.

The socio-historical formation of Brazil

The implementation of a European culture in a vast territory like Brazil, with natural conditions somewhat hostile and strange, was, in Holanda's opinion (1936), the crucial event of the early Brazilian colonization. Brazil's cultural formation involves, since the beginning, a contrast between the European culture, the expectations of the settlers towards the lands beyond the sea in contrast to the colony's ambivalent necessity to respond to them. The Brazilian people reveal, through identification issues, their conflict around the question of whether its culture might or might not be a mere reproduction of foreign influences. From the European point of view, the discovery of the Americas created a "utopian project", cherished during a "crepuscular moment" in the transition of the Middle Ages to Renaissance, when European navigators envisioned the discovery of a New World and medieval traditions were giving way to modernity (Holanda, 1936). Among many points of view, the myth of "Earthly Paradise", quoted by Souza (1994), was chosen in order to reveal the origin of the creation of a particular apparatus: namely, "apparatus of exoticism", present in the Brazilian foundation matrix. The myth of "Earthly Paradise" was initially allocated in African or Eastern lands and used to feed the European "imagination" since the sixth century. Discovering lands in the New World transferred the European expectations to the lands located under the equator line, where, in a sinless world, the promise of "uncommon sensual ecstasies" was mixed up with the nature's lushness and richness in gold and precious stones (Souza, 1994). Thus, the projection of the European utopia upon America, the "Edenic myth", produced various consequences, following each colonising enterprise, creating different social organisations. While the Puritan settlers from New England had transferred themselves to America, breaking the bonds with their mother country where they were persecuted, the Iberian settlers travelled to America as legal representatives of their Crowns. The particularities of both Protestant and Catholic religions emphasised the differences even more, allowing many translations for the "Earthly Paradise". The myth had the connotation of moral and spiritual faith challenge in British America, while in Iberian America it meant the vision of paradise *in loco*. This latter view developed itself differently in Hispanic America, through the image of an abundance of mineral wealth.

As for Brazil, little option was left to the Portuguese navigators, after docking in the Brazilian land and witnessing the exotic vegetation and the naked native indigenous people, but the confirmation that they had arrived at the "Earthly Paradise" indeed. Hence, an immediate interpretation of the myth of "Earthly Paradise" in Iberian America "ended up pushing Brazil towards the erotic option, the search of personal satisfaction through emotional relationships with other people" (Souza, 1994, p. 65). To the Portuguese, the "wondrous" translated itself to sex and, through the influences of Romanticism during the nineteenth century, ended up turning into "exoticism".

Holanda, in "Roots of Brazil" (1936), introduces a psychological analysis of Brazilian social formation since the beginning of the Portuguese colonisation. It combines, in a very original way, the negligence of the Portuguese, the indigenous people's idleness and incapacity for manual labour, and the exploitation of the African slavery. The Brazilian cultural heritage arose through the particularities of an Iberian culture that is the most decisive trace of Hispanic evolution in America. Indeed, due to the historical differences between Iberian and Anglo-Saxon nations, different translations of the above-mentioned aspects of the settlers' ideals and in their correspondent "foundation matrices" can be found in America.

The independence and the cult of idleness, the loose social structure and the lack of an organised hierarchy, characteristics of the Portuguese society, encouraged anarchic elements in the colony, typical of incohesion processes (Hopper, 2003a), all omnipresent in Brazilian society. Those circumstances ended up building a society based on solidarity and friendship bonds, rather than formal or profitable activities. It is important to highlight that Protestantism's ideas and values, such as order and labour's morality, had little effect on the cultural formation of Iberian countries. The Catholic principles favoured the development of a more universal or less exclusive ethics. While the new Protestants used to glorify the associative work of individualistic character, among Iberian nations the predominant attitude was "the idleness to the detriment of business and the prevalence of contemplative life in opposition to productive activity" (Holanda, 1936, p. 48, translated for this edition). Thus, at the same time that a rigidly hierarchised society was built in Brazil, a rejection or denial of the state's legislative and impersonal codes has also been developed. Consequently, doctrines such as patriarchy, culture of personalism, exaltation of personal and cordial values have always been highly valued in Brazilian society.

The process of colonisation in Brazil was characterised by strong exploitation of its natural resources. Until 1808, when the Portuguese Royal Family moved its Court to Brazil, this was an essentially agrarian country where, initially, sugarcane was grown in large plantations—the *latifundium*. Manpower was supplied by African slaves, since the native indigenous people resisted manual work (considered a feminine task). Such peculiarities strengthened a rural elite and the construction of a rigidly hierarchised, patriarchal society. Modernity in Brazil arrived together with the Portuguese Royal Family's immigration. The royals brought in their "luggage" habits of the aristocracy, their institutions, and the bourgeois way of living to a country of pre-feudal characteristics. Holanda (1936) points out that the sugar mills' owners created a unique society in history founded upon self-sufficient power structures, and independent from surrounding emerging cities, unlike the ones in the developing Medieval Europe. Therefore, Brazilian social development has always been guided by the huge authoritarian power from the rural complex to the detriment of modern and bourgeoisie-orientated organisation of the metropolis. This particular concept in history indirectly influenced the Brazilian way of living, justifying the coexistence in its society of contradictory patterns strongly imbedded in Brazilian social unconscious. On the one hand, a highly hierarchised, authoritarian and complementary society was developed, with explicit norms of morality and individuality. On the other hand, the egalitarian and individualistic ideals of the Brazilian "late modernity", which are actually *"para inglês ver"* (literally, "to be seen by an Englishman") is an aphorism that sums up a common attitude of establishing rules that are not meant to be obeyed. Schwarcz (2008) agrees with Holanda (1936) when he affirms that this implicit double-reference code has always been an obstacle to the development of capitalism in Brazil. The concentration of power in the hands of the rural elite, who control regional political parties, consolidated "a mentality which is the historical outcome of the mixture of liberalism with agrarianism, rather than a geographic determinism or environment imposition" (Holanda, 1936, p. 59, translated for this edition). Therefore, the metropolis would simply be an extension of the countryside, bearing marks and carrying vices in an embarrassing continuum.

Therefore, the persistence of structures of intimacy and cordiality based on the so-called "primary contacts"—heart or blood bonds—in Brazilian society end up imposing private values on public domain. As a result, the relationships with institutions are rather loose. There is an implicit reluctance to "formalism"—both characteristics of rational hierarchies of egalitarian societies—and a resistance to adopting certain aspects of democratic ideals (Schwarcz, 2008). This conjuncture led to the creation of Holanda's (1936) myth of the "cordial man", an image largely disseminated in the Brazilian culture, summarising the essence of Brazilian people. Holanda's cordiality is far from common sense and is often misinterpreted. It translates the Brazilians' incapacity to deal with political and citizenship issues. Cordiality has nothing to do with kindness: on the contrary, it reveals the Brazilians' aversion to both formalism and social conventionalism. Amiability, hospitality to foreigners, and generosity are all definitive traits of Brazilian personality, which are attributed to centuries of active, prolific, and persistent ancestral influence of coexistence patterns, shaped in the rural and patriarchal Brazilian atmospheres. The cordial man is spontaneous and keeps innate his emotions. Closeness in dealing with strangers and aversion to social distances and formalism reveal how Brazilians absorbed the conflict between the demands of the internal and external worlds and constituted a "personality", a character (Fenichel, 1946) which led them to implant private values into the public sphere. Thus, the myth of the "cordial man" represents "the Brazilian character", established in the complex interplay of ancestral psychological and sociological processes. Additionally, cordiality involves the reproduction and the preservation of power relations and retrograde socio-political structures.

Gilberto Freyre (1936), eminent sociologist and disciple of Boas, provided a vast comprehension of the Brazilian agrarian and patriarchal structure. Among his many contributions, one stands out—his work on ethnic plurality and racial composition in the history of Brazil. The idea of "racial democracy" is essential for the construction of various myths and phantasies in the Brazilian social unconscious. This phenomenon takes us to an apparatus of power, the "apparatus of miscegenation" (Tadei, 2002), which demystifies the "natural" and naïve views of racial composition in Brazil. The concept of miscegenation is taken from the Latin *miscere* "to mix" + *genus* "race", "kind", meaning the mixing of different racial groups through marriage, cohabitation, sexual relations, and procreation (*Etymology Dictionary*, 2013).

In Freyre's (1936) opinion, the Portuguese settler, due to his hybrid racial and social formation (the product of historical Muslim influence), was predisposed to miscegenation, and, thus, more easily accepted the mixture of races that constitutes the Brazilian people. Historically, in Portuguese colonies, interracial marriage was supported by the Court, which found in the admixture of races a way to boost low populations, thus ensuring a successful and cohesive settlement (Schwarcz, 1998). One of the consequences of these policies for Brazilian society was that the idea that being composed by a "mixture of races" was always met with acceptance, revealing a peculiar and positive trait that became engrained in the Brazilian foundation matrix. According to historical data, the marriage between the Portuguese settler Diogo Alvares Correa (called *Caramuru*) and the *Tupinambá* indigenous princess (called *Paraguaçu*, later baptised in France with the name Katherine du Brézil), was the first documented interracial marriage in Brazil. This union, occurring in the sixteenth century, gave birth to the first Brazilian family. Its history is surrounded by several myths present in the Brazilian foundation matrix (Doria, 2000). The legends and narratives about the mixed marriage of *Caramuru* and *Paraguaçu* are in tune with the policies fostered by the Portuguese colonies in favour of interracial marriages. They also exemplify some aspects of racial fantasies and the primal scene of miscegenation rooted in the social unconscious of particular societies (Hopper, 2008).

The concept of miscegenation is tied to concepts of racial difference, diverging globally as well as historically, depending on cultural perceptions and socio-political circumstances. Unlike other countries in which the concept of miscegenation was avoided, in Brazil the idea of multi-raciality found a special place in the development of Brazilian visions of its own breed. If, in Nazi Germany, "race-mixing" was banned (Nuremberg Laws, 1935–1945), and in countries such as the USA and South Africa anti-miscegenation laws prevailed until recent years, prohibiting and criminalising interethnic marriages, in Brazil the idea of admixture of races has always been valued and seen in a positive and unique way. So, even acknowledging that the term miscegenation sounds problematic outside Brazil, and words like "hybridisation", "cross-breeding", "blending" might express more comfortably the idea of Brazilian mixture of races or cultures for an

English reader, these words do not fit with the Brazilian cultural context.

Another possibility could be the use of the word *mestizaje*, *mestiçagem*, *métissage* applied in Spanish, Portuguese, and French. Older than miscegenation (a word created only in the nineteenth century), *mestizaje* is derived from the Late Latin *mixticius* for "mixed", which is also the root of the Spanish word *mestizo* (*Etymology Dictionary*, 2013). The word *mestizaje* expresses not only the "fusion of races or cultures, but is also related to the idea of the creation of a new identity, born of fusion, including a pride invested in phenomenon" (Tubert-Oklander & Hopper, 2013, personal communication). However, in Portuguese, the word *miscigenação*, derived from the same Latin root as the English word, was never considered offensive as its English version "miscegenation" was, although it has been historically tied to the caste system established during the colonial era in Spanish-speaking Latin America (Maio & Santos, 1996). Thus, even with so many negative contents in other cultures, the word employed by Brazilian scholars to describe the phenomenon is miscegenation.

In Brazil conceptualisations such as "Earthly Paradise", "There is no sin south of the Equator", are attributed to the country, to cordial relationships, and to loosening of racial prejudice, and have all contributed to the formation of a social culture privileging ethnic mixture and both religious and cultural syncretism. Tadei (2002) believes that Freyre's (1936) ideas were significant to the trivialisation of the miscegenation idea, transforming it into an inevitable and unquestionable fact. Nevertheless, he stresses that such a characteristic should be analysed within the Portuguese colonisation project for the country, as this historical formation would respond to an apparatus of power:

> Such apparatus ended up establishing certain rationality in our country, for it is accepted as an elementary structure, found in every discursive work produced about our country and our national identity. It can be understood as an elementary discursive structure that determines our way of thinking about Brazil and the Brazilian problem. (Tadei, 2002, p. 3, translated for this edition)

Actually, the "apparatus of miscegenation" involves a pool of knowledge and strategies that influence the national identity, deeply rooted in the Brazilian foundation matrix. The apparatus target is the integration of, and rendering docile, the various ethnic groups that are on the roots of the Brazilian nationality, making markedly different elements of society appear more consistent, generating docile, poorly delimitated, and politically manipulable subjectivities.

The genesis of the Brazilian ethnic issue must be understood through stages, which initially involve the knowledge favourable to miscegenation. Such knowledge came from the colonial religious environment, continuing until its epistemologisation and reinterpretation during the nineteenth and twentieth centuries. During this last phase, the idea of "racial democracy" was consolidated, emerging in the figure of the "mestizo", who distinguishes himself as someone better adapted for the life in the tropics. Actually, the "mestizo" would combine, in a unique way, favourable attributes for life in the colony and would carry in him an "evolution" when compared with the native people and the black slave.

Thus, miscegenation became an idealised characteristic which was quickly turned into a social nexus amid the various ethnicities of Brazilian population. As miscegenation promotes ethnic mixture, it erases the origins, the past, and contradictions of Brazilian people who, turned to the future, get rid of resistances as well as individual and national historical roots. Besides, miscegenation favours the mercantilist, political, and intellectual viewpoints and solves manpower and religious moral problems. The immigration of white Europeans at the end of the nineteenth century completes the picture, providing the additional white element for the territory's "Europeanisation". Results can be found to the present day in controversial and discussed issues on national identity, the kaleidoscope of races, and distinct cultures that actually interpenetrate themselves.

The theoretical base for discussing the miscegenation issue was, for a long time, "social Darwinism" and "evolutionism". Nevertheless, contributions by Artur Ramos, Gilberto Freyre, and Jorge Amado favourably transferred the issue from the purely racial/biological sphere to the cultural level. Through the celebration of the encounter and the mixture of ethnicities and cultures that constitutes the Brazilian people, these authors managed to turn previously considered negative aspects into positive ones, contributing, however, to the propagation of the "apparatus of miscegenation".

Both the abolition of slavery and the proclamation of the Republic marked, by the end of the nineteenth century, the demise of agrarian dominance and brought changes to the national political scene. The Brazilian state consolidated itself with a modern face, inspired by the ideals of the French Revolution, an event that influenced the history of the independent Ibero-American nations. With the state's emancipation and its rupture with European guardianship, the current principles were then acquired and reinterpreted according to the old colonial and rural patterns, generating the implementation of changes that, according to Holanda (1936), were related more to appearance than to real meaning. That is, the implementation of democratic ideals in the country denotes the survival of the old colonial and patriarchal order, with all its moral, social, and political consequences. Unfortunately, our status as an independent country has not yet been able to eradicate these outcomes.

Then, in the twentieth century, a revolutionary cultural movement—the Anthropophagic Movement—took place and introduced an important characteristic of the Brazilian foundation matrix, strongly linked to the discussion about the "apparatus of miscegenation" and the search for national identity. It preached the idea of self-enrichment of the Brazilian culture through anthropophagism (cannibalism)—to devour and incorporate aspects of the various cultures present in its formation (Candido, 1981). The Brazilian Modernist Movement had its climax during the Week of Modern Art of 1922, representing a real revolution in Brazilian artistic language. It gathered artists such as the writer, Oswald de Andrade, who introduced the anthropological view of the Brazilian as "the civilised anthropophagous". The renewal of art was born of the retaking of native indigenous values, the release of instincts, and the celebration of naïveté. Undoubtedly, the "Anthropophagic Movement" disturbed the Brazilian imitational behaviour of European patterns, granting a new face to Brazilian art. However, due to its characteristics, the movement had its basis still quite tied to the pitfalls of the "apparatuses of power". Its proposed alternatives to the Brazilian culture ended up strengthening them. The consequence of such policies, in subjective terms, was the impression that the Brazilian people seem to conjugate the exoticism of the European vision with an "Edenic sensuality". This vision that Brazilians seem to have of themselves is found in both the "personality" of the cordial man, and in the ideal types (Weber) represented by the rogue and the mulatto.

From the 1960s onwards, we have been observing normative changes, as well as new forms of western capitalism. The decline of patriarchy, fading of traditions, the sexual revolution, changes in morals and ethics, and the growing power of science have all contributed to weakening traditional institutions and also triggered transformations in the world of symbolic references (Bauman, 1997). Thus, the presence of a series of political and social changes were found in western societies which, when inserted into a globalised world, remapped borders and reconfigured spaces, providing the public and private spheres with new contours (Sennett, 1974).

The economy, the industry, the cities' huge populations, and the rural exodus of the contemporary Brazil barely resemble the agrarian structure of the past. The consequence of this process was the appearance of huge socio-economic inequalities. The contrast between the archaic and the new, the old structures and the contemporary world, generate the main social conflicts today, clashes that find their main outlet in violence. From the 1970s onwards, the culture of narcissism (Lasch, 1979) found wide acceptance in the private sphere due to the disillusionment with political ideals and the substitution of ethics of work for those of consumption. In the public sphere, however, cordiality and patriarchy coexist side by side with economic liberalism and capitalism. Brazilian culture, although preserving the richness of Brazilian tradition, the syncretism in religion, and the joys of carnival and football, shows a considerable "Americanisation" and globalisation, leading Brazilians to affirm that on many occasions the society may be reduced to its exotic and caricatured aspects, a "product for export".

The foundation matrix of Brazil and the Brazilian social unconscious

Many aspects of the formation of the culture of Brazil can be understood in the context of strategies for individual and cultural survival by the Brazilian people in face of their fear of annihilation in response to many traumatogenic processes (Hopper, 1991). In a country in which territorial vastness naturally led to processes of incohesion (Hopper, 2003a), national cohesion was achieved through mechanisms of coercive power that led to the near extinction of the indigenous population and to centuries of slavery's systemic oppression. Nevertheless, in spite of the fact that the violence against "the weaker" was one of the main elements constituting the social formation of Brazil, it did not lead, as it did in other countries, to major revolutions or to armed struggle, although several bloody episodes were a part of the country's history. In Brazil, these difficulties were repressed and denied and the survival of the population was guaranteed in a creative way through the ideal types that, in a caricature and disguised, but also immature, manner, through unique laws and codes of behaviour, instead of facing the oppression, used it to resist.

The cordial man, the rogue, and the mulatto are "character" types (Fenichel, 1946) created and co-created by the Brazilian foundation matrix. Conjugating instinctual demands and adaptations to the demands of a hostile external environment, they dodged and denied traumatic experiences, establishing themselves as a subtle force widespread in the country, capable of reverting to, and reinventing, codes and patterns of communication and behaviour. However, in spite of their versatility, these types of character are captured and imprisoned in the demands of the apparatuses of power, not presenting characteristics that make it possible to associate them with the maturity or the independence of the "revolutionary character", described by Fromm (1963) and developed in group analysis by Hopper (2003b). Thus, whereas "the revolutionary character must be able to make the social unconscious conscious" (Hopper, 2003b, p. 151), these Brazilian character types only reproduce the constraints and the restraints of the social unconscious.

The "cordial man", or "Do you know who I am?"?

It is possible to observe, in Brazilian historical–cultural formation, many common characteristics of Latin and Mediterranean societies, where hierarchical systems with egalitarian and individualistic ideals coexist in apparent harmony. In this regard, the myth of the "cordial man" was exploited by Da Matta (1986) to represent a system of practices adopted by the Brazilian people involving a double code of social, political, and ideological coexistence. On one hand, the traditional segments, the patriarchy and the personalism, are a product of the colonial system regulating personal relationship. On the other hand, the modern state's laws prevail. In Brazil, the balance tips in favour of the first segment, mainly due to the strong presence of private norms in the public domain. Due to this fact, the appreciation of the reign of charity and goodwill leads to the detriment of egalitarianism in relation to the state's laws. According to Da Matta (1986), the persistence of such a double code reveals itself in the typical behaviour defined as "*o jeitinho brasileiro*" (the Brazilian way) and in the frequent use of the adage—"Do you know who I am?" Such practices are used as bargaining tools in many ordinary situations where the real intention is to neutralise the principle of impersonality and enforce old hierarchic codes of the colonial system. This behaviour presupposes the neutralisation of the exotic vision of the "cordial Brazilian" who, although apparently modern, democratic, and docile, carries the mark of authoritarianism and class hierarchy. In reality, these behaviours reveal ethical issues, reproducing and modernising old power relationships between the coloniser and the colonised.

The apparatus of exoticism

The "apparatus of exoticism" is intrinsically related to the national identity, with the image Brazilians build of themselves and the image foreigners have of them. The celebration of the exotic by Brazilians was a way to respond to the settler's utopian mandate in Brazil. This identification forced Brazilians to look for an exotic national significant through which they could ratify their difference (Tadei, 2002). Souza (1994) carried out a provocative psychoanalytic analysis of such apparatus, assuming that the way the Europeans found to approach something they regarded as different, beautiful, and exciting in Brazil was through the idea of the "uncanny" (Freud, 1919h). He affirms that although the "uncanny" does not provoke any aesthetic feeling to the observer's eyes, it causes anxiety instead, due to the return of the repressed. In Brazil, a transformation of such a mechanism occurred. To Souza (1994), the "uncanny" is an apparatus that carries the capacity to attribute to the other (the stranger), something uncomfortably familiar (intimate) to oneself. As a defence against the threat provoked by the "uncanny"—and here the fear of annihilation may be conjured—the observer regards as beautiful and exciting what caused strangeness before. Reassuring himself of his subjective axis, this defence substitutes the passivity of the anxiety experienced for the activity of aesthetic admiration. The approach of the stranger through the prism of exoticism reveals *"to be the way found to dominate the strangeness and threat represented by the uncanny . . . this is the psychic possibility of covering the object's fantastic crudity with an image of narcissistic origin"* (Souza, 1994, p. 130, translated for this edition).

Hence, the exoticism is a way cultures have to pre-organise the subject's narcissistic recapture, every time he is confronted with the uncanny, in the form of the stranger (Souza, 1994). In Brazil's culture, it is possible to affirm that its people find themselves seduced by the western demand for exoticism. The danger of such seduction lies in the fact that "exoticism neutralises people's political competence though aestheticisation" (Souza, 1994, p. 132, translated for this edition). According to the western view, the official culture needs the exotic as an object of study and delight in order to depoliticise its existence. Thus, due to the confluence of cultures in the formation of Brazilian society, the lack of engrained traditions and the European view on exoticism, the Brazilian perceives and responds to his cultural peculiarities with this same approach.

However, to Souza (1994), exoticism is not the only a dominating strategy used towards the stranger. Racism is another possibility, as we will see next. Instead of using aesthetical mediations to disguise unconscious phantasies, they are manifested through it.

The apparatus of miscegenation

The racial issue in Brazil is rather peculiar, quite different from other nations where a past of enslavement recalls violence and abuse. In Brazil, history has been recast in a positive and defensive way. Freyre's myth of "social democracy" and the Brazilian's "natural predisposition" to miscegenation took the racial issue off of the social–political agenda. Indeed, it is possible to affirm that the apparatus of miscegenation fulfilled its role. According to Schwarcz, in Brazil two different realities coexist: "on the one hand, the discovery of a country of miscegenated beliefs and customs and on the other, a place of invisible racism and a hierarchy deeply rooted in its intimacy" (Schwarcz, 1998, p. 241, translated for this edition). The "apparatus of miscegenation" seems to have bequeathed to us repressed, or even internalised, prejudices such as the idea that, due to the mestizo character, there is a hardly cohesive, badly delimited subjectivity.

To Tadei (2002), the Brazilian "apparatus of miscegenation" encourages ethnic mixing, puts sexuality in the strategic position of an instrument capable of promoting ethnic confraternity, dilutes the national identity, and, thus, consolidates itself in an amalgam that gathers various national elements and then manoeuvres this identity in specific directions. The "apparatus of miscegenation" is, therefore, planted in the foundations of Brazilian social unconscious, deeply rooted in its foundation matrix, for its roots lie in both in Brazil's remote past and in the troubles faced during the colonial period which forced different ethnic groups to carry on activities of exploitation.

After the Second World War, UNESCO promoted research about Brazilian racial relations, questioning the myth of "racial democracy", and revealed the existence of racial prejudices in the country. The data pointed out the interconnections between social inequalities, race, and poverty (Maio & Santos, 1996). More contemporary analysis of the effects of the "racial democracy" in Brazil revealed how the "apparatus of miscegenation" allowed the denial of racial issues. Fortunately, the birth of "negro movements" is dismantling the pitfalls created in the past (Rufino, 1996). Thus, race remains an important contemporary topic to explore in the Brazilian social unconscious.

The mestizo

"Brazil is the hell of the black, the purgatory of the white and the paradise of the mulattoes" (Ramos, 1934, translated for this edition).

Through the paradisiacal interpretation of miscegenation as exemplifying a "confraternity of races", which presumes the celebration of sexuality as a factor capable of integrating the ethnic groups, the idealised image of the "mestizo" arose to describe a person who gathers the characteristics that better adapt to Brazilian life. Nevertheless, the insidious aspect of the "mestizo" is the fact that several prejudices and "social Darwinism" ended up being validated in the country by the "apparatus of miscegenation" which celebrates the traits derived from the ethnic mixture. Actually, the "mestizo" is the result of the view that Brazilians are hybrid and exotic beings. The purpose of the idealisation of the mestizo is to avoid confrontation between colonisers and colonised through the neutralisation of traditional characteristics of the various ethnic groups that compose the Brazilian population. The result obtained through miscegenation is cultural assimilation and a homogenisation that leads to de-rooting and production of controllable subjectivities. Brazilian society itself, unaware of the strength of these "apparatuses of power", regards the figure of the "mestizo" as a product of a defensive and "natural" evolution of a Brazilian race that endured centuries of oppression and authoritarianism.

If, on the one hand, the homogenisation of races in Brazil produced the praised mestizo as a character who was able to amalgamate cultural differences through unconscious power-relations strategies (produced against the fear of annihilation), on the other hand, it is possible to attribute to miscegenation processes the flourishing of creativity and diversity in the country. Thus, the mestizo character, "product of the apparatus of miscegenation", contributed to the creation of a vibrant Brazilian melting pot, a creative mixture of cultures, races, and diversity.

The rogue

The construction of a character, the Brazilian rogue, gathers a mixture of traits attributed to the "cordial man" and to the "mestizo", introducing the possibility of relativisation of laws and customs in a restricted world of bourgeois morality and rigid rules. The "rogue", probably a "mestizo", points at other dimensions, taking us to a world of compensations, the world of the "*jeitinho brasileiro*" (Brazilian way), bringing solutions and celebrating behaviours that creatively break the laws without questioning the *status quo*. The "rogue" reveals the power of the weak and the oppressed, pointing in the direction of strategies that glorify the creative individual solution, protecting the individual from the oppression of the systems of power.

Discussion

The investigation of the Brazilian social unconscious through "apparatuses of power" made possible the understanding of not only the role of such mechanisms in the construction of the Brazilian social system, but the effect of both exoticism and miscegenation on its formation. It was possible to observe how behaviour and communication patterns, myths, denials, and other forms of unconscious defences were actually strategies of survival. These processes were ways people found in the culture and in the social system to protect themselves against the fear of individual and collective annihilation by other races seen as "superior" during the colonial times and after the immigration wave at the end of the nineteenth century. Brazil exhibits, contrary to any other culture (notably those where immigration and a frightening mixture of races threatened the countries' socio-cultural formation), a well-liked and valued cultural assimilation which has turned the country into a kaleidoscope of different races and cultures. Thereby, it appears that Brazil has opted for a peculiar kind of resistance to domination by means of an unconscious defence mechanism against the settlement process: instead of resisting the violent and traumatic contact with other cultures or even antagonising such contact, it has denied the existence of oppositions or racial and cultural conflicts, choosing instead the assimilation and "anthro-pophagic" incorporation of its disparities. The positive side of this process made of Brazil an attractive and peculiarly cohesive country, allowing Brazilians to carry with them the phantasy, supported by "apparatuses of power", of being a unique people of a plural and anthropophagic culture, unequalled in its richness of traces and languages.

In Brazil, the "apparatuses of power" generated an image of a joyful and docile people and of a society with characteristics and types of strong, popular appeal. Nevertheless, the appearance of globalised values, the impact of contemporary culture, and transformations in subjectivities have weakened the efficiency of such "apparatuses", emphasising their negative aspects or even the disintegration of many of their mechanisms. Thus, as Le Roy (1994) claims, rapid changes are taking place in all cultures and tendencies of dilution, fragmentation, and decay can be observed, bringing impairment not only into sym-bolic structures—which proved to be both insufficient and inconsis-tent—but also to the "continent" of the entire social system (Le Roy, 1994, p. 193). These considerations move the axis of analysis in tradi-tionally idealised Brazilian social cohesion to its appreciation from the standpoint of incohesion processes (Hopper, 2003b). The "apparatuses of power", rooted and co-constructed in the Brazilian foundation matrix, guarantee a "continent" throughout the Brazilian cultural formation (Le Roy, 1994) and an unimaginable cohesion in such a vast and unequal country. Nevertheless, if, on the one hand, the strategy of survival founded by Brazilians against the fear of annihilation guaranteed national sovereignty and a fictitious cohesion led to the standardisation of different aspects of the culture, on the other hand, it did not fail to reveal patterns of interaction, normation, communication, and styles of thinking and feeling predominant in Hopper's (2003a) fourth basic assumption: Incohesion: Aggregation/Massification.

In general, bi-polar states of aggregation and massification can be found in the cultural formation of Brazil. Phenomena of "Disarroy and me-ness", typical of states of aggregation, are seen in the behaviour of the rogue and the cordial man. Similarly, the racial democracy, miscegenation, cultural assimilation, and the anthropophagic culture reveal processes of fusion and homogenisation, predominant in the states of massification. Aggressiveness is another relevant aspect and the violence previously restrained or neutralised by the action of the apparatuses of power is now everywhere, supporting the culture of deviance and anomie. The land of joy, carnival, and football also reveals itself to be the land of the "urban guerilla" and a certain lack of ethics in public life. In Brazil's contemporary world, patriarchal and cultural values have been replaced by social disintegration, destitution, and violence. As a consequence, one can notice a double movement in Brazilian society: on the one hand, fostered by a long hierarchical tradition of the colonial system, strongly engrained in our "foundation matrix", it is possible to verify an exacerbation of individual interests, similar to the "culture of narcissism" (Lasch, 1979). "Individualism", the Brazilian personalism, is employed as a defence and self-affirmation mechanism of the individual and his interest in the face of a society of weak codes and ambiguous laws. In the absence of constraints, individual values prevail as a form of protection of either the individual or the nuclear family from the absence of a "good enough" containing frame in the social evidencing of characteristics of aggregation. On the other hand, a new middle class has originated from the less economically favoured segments of the population and is recently emerging in Brazil due to various governmental incentive policies, gradually achieving status and purchasing power. This change foreshadows the appearance of a new socio-economic configuration based on more democratic and egalitarian patterns.

Apparently, such policies propitiate a new approach towards the country's social system that seems to distance itself from Brazil's patriarchy, but it is still too early to determine both the positive and negative aspects of such policies.

Concluding comment

Throughout this chapter, it was possible to identify how the Brazilian social unconscious was structured and, above all, how the efforts towards cohesion of the disparate aspects of its culture were outlined through "apparatuses of power" and defensive phantasies. The way such "apparatuses" managed to amalgamate aspects of Brazil's cultural formation, plus the way they established an order in which the persistent incohesion and frailty of national identity was dealt with, created a unique culture. Indeed, those "apparatuses" did protect the country from fragmentation, allowing the coexistence of diversities and heterogeneities in a single huge territory. Nevertheless, it is important to remember that the social processes and the dynamics of the social unconscious are constantly mutating. Thus, there are many questions that could be asked, and the answers are yet to come, but, meanwhile, we should remember that Brazil is a young country still in development.

References

Bauman, Z. (1997). *Post Modernity and Discontents*. Cambridge: Polity Press.

Candido, A. (1981). *Formação da Literatura Brasileira* [Brazilian Literature Formation]. Belo Horizonte: Itatiaia.

Da Matta, R. (1986). *O que faz o Brasil, Brasil?* [What Makes Brazil, Brazil?]. Rio de Janeiro: Ed. Rocco.

Dalal, F. (1998). *Taking the Group Seriously: Towards a Post-Foulkesian Group Analytic Theory*. London: Jessica Kingsley.

Doria, F. (2000). *Caramuru e Catarina: lendas e narrativas sobre a Casa da Torre de Garcia D'Avila* [Caramuru and Catarina: Legends and Narratives about Garcia D'Avila's Tower House]. São Paulo: Ed. SENAC.

Etymology Dictionary. www.etymonline.com/index.php?term=miscegenation (accessed 15 December 2013).

Fenichel, O. (1946). *The Psychoanalytic Theory of Neurosis*. New York: Routledge.

Foucault, M. (1979). *Microfísica do Poder* [Microphysics of Power]. Rio de Janeiro: Graal.

Freud, S. (1919h). The 'uncanny'. *S. E.*, *17*: 217–256. London: Hogarth.

Freyre, G. (1933). *Casa Grande e Senzala* [The Mansions and the Shanties]. São Paulo: José Olimpio.

Fromm, E. (1963). The revolutionary character. In: *The Dogma of Christ* (pp. 122–139). New York: Holt, Rinehart and Winston.

Holanda, B. S. (1936) *As Raízes do Brasil* [The Brazilian Roots]. Rio de Janeiro: Companhia das Letras.

Hopper, E. (1991). Encapsulation as a defense against the fear of annihilation. *International Journal of Psychoanalysis*, *72*(4): 607–624..

Hopper, E. (2003a). *Traumatic Experience in the Unconscious Life of Groups*. London: Jessica Kingsley.

Hopper, E. (2003b). *The Social Unconscious: Selected Papers*. London: Jessica Kingsley.

Hopper, E. (2008). On racial fantasies and the primal scene of miscegenation. *International Journal of Psychoanalysis*, *89*(4): 1220–1221.

Hopper, E., & Weinberg, H. (2011). *The Social Unconscious in Persons, Groups and Societies: Mainly Theory*. London: Karnac.

Lasch, C. (1979). *Culture of Narcissism*. New York: Warner, 1990.

Le Roy, J. (1994). Group-analysis and culture. In: D. Brown & L. Zinkin (Eds.), *The Psyche and the Social World* (pp. 180–201). London: Jessica Kingsley.

Maio, M., & Santos, R. (Eds.) (1996). *Raça, Ciência e Sociedade* [Race, Science and Society]. Rio de Janeiro: Editora Fio Cruz, CCBB.

Ramos, A. (1934). *O Negro brasileiro* [The Brazilian Negro]. Recife: Fundação Joaquim Nabuco, 1988.

Rufino, J. (1996). O negro como lugar [The Negro as a Place]. In: M. Maio & R. Santos (Eds.), *Raça, Ciência e Sociedade* [Race, Science and Society] (pp. 219–231). Rio de Janeiro: Editora Fio Cruz, CCBB.

Schwarcz, L. M. (1998). *O Espetáculo das Raças* [The Spectacle of Races]. São Paulo: Companhia das Letras.

Schwarcz, L. M. (2008). Buarque de Holanda e essa tal de "cordialidade" [Buarque de Holanda and the so-called cordiality]. *IDE, Psicanálise e Cultura*, *31*(46): 83–89.

Sennett, R. (1974). *The Fall of the Public Man*. New York: W. W. Norton.

Souza, O. (1994). *Fantasias de Brasil* [Brazilian Fantasies]. São Paulo: Escuta.

Tadei, E. M. (2002). A Mestiçagem enquanto um dispositivo de poder e a identidade nacional [The *Mestizage* as an apparatus of power and the national identity]. *Psicologia Ciência e Profissão*, 22(4): 2–13.

Tubert-Oklander, J., & Hopper, E. (2013). Personal communication concerning "miscegenation, hybridisation and mestizage".

INDEX